JOE LA POMPE

COPY PASTE

HOW ADVERTISING RECYCLES IDEAS

HOW TO BE ORIGINAL?

BY MARK TUNGATE

MARK TUNGATE

is a journalist, a book writer and the editorial director of the Epica Awards.

En

When I was thinking about how I'd tackle this job, my first idea was simply to copy the preface of the last edition. That would be funny and, of course, easy. I could disguise my laziness by saying it was an exercise in irony, or an homage, or – to stretch the point – merely a coincidence.

But no. Unfortunately, for those of us who regularly begin our day staring at a blank screen, the act of creation is hard. When considering the phrase "work of art", people tend to overlook the word "work". (I stole that quote from somebody, but I can't remember who.)

Creativity and originality tend to be mentioned in the same breath. But is any creative work truly original? Books, films, plays, song lyrics and indeed commercials tend to talk with one another. They are part of a long conversation that stretches back into the past. Most works of art, I would suggest, have a family tree that can be traced back for generations.

Star Wars, Harry Potter, James Bond – they all have their roots in far earlier creations, from fairy tales to Greek myths.

A couple of my favourite Italian authors have played around with the idea of intercreativity. Italo Calvino's *If On A Winter's Night A Traveler...* constructs an entire story from the opening pages of separate (imaginary) novels. And in *Foucault's Pendulum*, by Umberto Eco, a group of friends create a fake conspiracy theory by cobbling together elements of previous conspiracies.

A lot of creativity involves "cobbling together" – rearranging ideas and influences to form new and interesting patterns. It's the creator's voice, his or her own interpretation, that gives the resulting work its original feel and texture.

We see this approach to creativity in music, too. One of my favourite singers is Frank Sinatra. A crooner rather than a songwriter, Sinatra interpreted the work of others. He performed songs that had often been sung many times before, by many other people. But Sinatra's voice was unique.

So perhaps an act of creativity doesn't have to be entirely original. It's the same song, interpreted in a new way. Jazz is not theft. (I stole that idea from someone else, too. If you have any idea who, please let me know.)

But everything I've written until now is merely a sophisticated excuse. We all know originality when we see it. The temperature in the room changes; we feel a frisson. As editorial director of the Epica Awards (the only global creative prize awarded by advertising journalists) I see this all the time. I'm the one who presents the entries to the jury – and I watch their reactions.

By the way, the author of this book is on the jury too, so he can warn us if an entry is not entirely original. A brief debate about interpretation and coincidence inevitably follows. But the jury members are an experienced bunch – many of them have been writing about commercial creativity for half their lives – so they are allergic to repetition and laziness. They literally sit up in their seats when they see something new. Occasionally they applaud.

Which brings us to the big question. The ultimate question, at least in our industry. How do you create something original?

If I knew, I'd be working on it right now. At the risk of sounding trite, I'd say it requires being as "you" as you can possibly be. Ideas, stories, images – there are billions of them out there. But there's only one you. So let your eccentric, unique self run riot.

Not a very original suggestion, perhaps. But I just write about advertising. I'll leave the creativity to you. ∎

̂COMMENT ÊTRE ORIGINAL?

PAR MARK TUNGATE

MARK TUNGATE
est un journaliste et auteur
de livres. Il est également
directeur éditorial des
Epica Awards.

**En réfléchissant à la manière d'aborder
ce travail, ma première idée a été de tout
simplement recopier la préface de la dernière
édition. Je me disais que ce serait marrant et,
évidemment, facile. L'idée était de déguiser ma
fainéantise en un exercice d'ironie, ou un hommage,
voire – histoire de pousser le vice –
une simple coïncidence.**

Et puis non. Malheureusement, pour ceux
d'entre nous qui commencent régulièrement leur
journée face à un écran blanc, l'acte de création
est difficile. Lorsqu'ils parlent d'œuvre d'art,
les gens ont une fâcheuse tendance à éclipser
le verbe «œuvrer». (J'ai piqué cette citation à
quelqu'un, mais impossible de me rappeler qui.)

Créativité et originalité sont considérées
comme allant de pair. Mais tout travail créatif
peut-il être considéré comme original? Livres, films,
pièces de théâtre, paroles de chansons et publicités
sont autant d'œuvres qui communiquent les unes
avec les autres. Ces créations font partie intégrante
d'une longue conversation qui remonte au passé.
Je pense que la plupart des œuvres d'art ont
un arbre généalogique qui peut être retracé sur
plusieurs générations.

Star Wars, Harry Potter, James Bond... tous ont
des racines issues de créations antérieures,
de contes de fées aux mythes grecs.

Deux de mes auteurs italiens préférés se sont
intéressés à la question de l'interactivité.
Dans *Si par une nuit d'hiver un voyageur*, Italo Calvino
construit tout un récit à partir des premières
pages de plusieurs nouvelles imaginaires. *Le Pendule
de Foucault* d'Umberto Eco met quant à lui en
scène un groupe d'amis qui crée une conspiration
en assemblant des éléments extraits de
conspirations antérieures.

Une grande partie de la créativité implique de
«bricoler»; de réarranger les idées et les influences
en vue de former des modèles innovants et
intéressants. C'est la voix du créateur ou de la créatrice,
son interprétation, qui donne à l'œuvre
toute son originalité et sa substance.

On retrouve cette même approche de la
créativité dans la musique. Frank Sinatra compte
parmi mes chanteurs favoris. Crooner plus qu'auteur,
Sinatra a interprété le travail des autres. Il a
chanté des chansons qui avaient été reprises
de nombreuses fois, par de nombreuses personnes.
Malgré cela, sa voix demeurait unique.

Peut-être faut-il en déduire qu'un acte de
créativité n'est pas tenu par une obligation
d'originalité totale. C'est la même chanson,
interprétée d'une nouvelle manière.
Le jazz n'est pas du vol. (J'ai encore piqué cette
idée à quelqu'un. Si vous avez la moindre idée
de qui, dites-le moi.)

Tout ce que j'ai écrit jusqu'ici est tout juste
une excuse sophistiquée. Nous reconnaissons
tous l'originalité en la voyant. C'est comme
si la température de la pièce changeait soudainement;
on ressent un frisson. En tant que directeur éditorial
des Epica Awards (la seule prix internationale
décernée par des journalistes spécialistes
de la publicité), j'en suis témoin au quotidien.
C'est à moi que revient la tâche de présenter
les candidatures au jury, et j'observe leurs réactions
à cet instant.

D'ailleurs, l'auteur de ce livre fait lui aussi
partie du jury, il pourra donc nous prévenir
si une œuvre n'est pas totalement originale.
Un court débat sur l'interprétation et la notion
de coïncidence suivra de manière inévitable.
Les membres du jury sont expérimentés:
bon nombre d'entre eux ont consacré leur vie
à écrire à propos de la créativité publicitaire.
Cela fait d'eux de grands allergiques à la
répétition et la fainéantise. Ils sont littéralement
debout sur leurs sièges lorsque quelque
chose de nouveau se présente à eux.
Parfois même, ils applaudissent.

Tout ceci nous amène à la grande question.
L'ultime question, du moins dans notre industrie.
Comment créer quelque chose d'original?

Si j'avais la réponse à cette question,
je serais en train de travailler dessus à l'heure
où je vous parle. Au risque de paraître banal,
je dirais qu'être original requiert d'être autant
vous-même que possible. Les idées, les histoires,
les images existent par milliards. En revanche,
il n'existe qu'une seule personne comme vous.
Alors laissez votre personnalité excentrique
et unique entamer sa propre émeute.

Le conseil n'est pas des plus originaux,
je le reconnais. Mais mon truc à moi, c'est d'écrire
à propos de la publicité. Pour ce qui est
de la créativité, je vous laisse ce rayon. ■

CONTENTS

SOMMAIRE

247 CAMPAIGNS / CAMPAGNES

En

With the green #hashtag, Joe invites you to take a stand, by giving your opinion online:

→ Visit *joelapompe.net*
→ In the search engine, enter the #hashtag
→ Coincidence or copycat? Be the judge.

Fr

Avec les #hashtag verts, Joe vous invite à prendre position, en donnant votre avis en ligne:

→ Rendez-vous sur *joelapompe.net*
→ Dans l'outil de recherche, entrez le #hashtag
→ Coïncidence ou copycat? Jugez en un clic.

WARNING BEFORE READING

JOE TALKS TO YOU

En

Hardly a day passes without a copycat case buzzing through social media. Hardly a day passes without an advertising agency hearing "that's already been done!", "déjà vu", "your idea reminds me of this or that". This topic is always a major concern among those working in the creative world, and leaves no one indifferent. Originality is a basic element of our work. And it is one of the reasons why achieving it prompts certain agencies to pay a lot for it. It is a major contributing factor to brand differentiation. It will surprise its audience, make a brand stand out and be remembered.

And yet, as strange as it may seem, a large number of campaigns sorely lack originality. In many cases they are just carbon copies of other campaigns. Stealing? Cheating? A lack of inspiration? An unconscious reminiscence? Free-riding? The aim of my approach is above all to precisely document and highlight this strange phenomenon, wish is often shamefully swept under the carpet. All too often, the creative world hides behind such statements as "we were unlucky" or "we didn't do it on purpose". I would like to take a hard-hitting visual approach aimed at stimulating debate and encouraging awareness. To avoid any misinterpretation of my intentions, here are a few fundamental things to know before I go into detail. I don't want this book to serve as inspiration. Instead, its purpose is to get you to ask the right questions before starting out on any creative project.

This book is not

A collection of "run-of-the-mill" ads. Far from it, the majority of the creations shown in this book have been presented at prestigious advertising festivals where they have gained awards for their originality. They have been sold for a high price by agencies claiming to be creative.

A settling of accounts. No particular brand, agency or person working in the creative sector is targeted. Whatever the country, whatever the period, we'll always find ads sorely lacking in originality. So this book is not a malicious accusation or an attack against a specific person or agency. The information in it is provided solely for the sake of precision and accuracy.

A value judgement. You would never hear me stating that the original must be better than the new version. All of the works presented feature exceptional quality. While some are plainly more original than others, the most accomplished and hardest-hitting are not always the ones that immediately come to mind.

The work of an anti-adman or another "ad-buster". I basically condemn these movements which are primarily caused – and I regret this – by an overdose of bad advertising. My book is critical and implacable, but I would like to see it as being constructive. It has been written by someone in love with intelligent and spectacular, but above all creative and innovative, ideas. I have masked my true identity to escape any influence or pressure. This mask is also a way of thumbing my nose at those oversized egos very often found in this walk of life, whose only concern is to see their names topping the tables.

An overall statement on all the multiple and varied sources of advertising inspiration. The book presents no campaign imitating or recycling a movie poster, the work of an illustrator or a work of art. What I do attack are the most absurd and grotesque ads: those which recycle other ads. Like a snake biting its own tail.

A university thesis on plagiarism and remembering ideas. The book's aim is not to examine all aspects of the issue, but rather to soundly illustrate the issue through visual evidence and open up a debate on it. I do not seek to justify, judge or punish but above all to inform and surprise.

This book is

A stock taking, a statement, a snapshot image of a phenomenon. I wanted to make it visual, easy to access and surprising – and not limited to traditional print advertising. What you get to see is merely my editorial choice, guided by my desire to be effective, to adapt as much as possible to the medium used and to work with what I know best. Obviously there is also a flagrant lack of originality in many online or mobile ads, and more generally in everything to do with creating logotypes, websites and graphics, but I had no intention of extending my scope that far.

The result of studying large amounts of documents and images, which involved many hours of work, of collecting and sorting information, whether in books, in databases or on the Internet.

An invitation to reflect: on ethical issues associated with the creative sector, on creative methods and on the influence of common culture. It raises a number of questions, some of which I will be mentioning at the end of this foreword. Please do not hesitate to send me yours via social media.

A playful way of rendering to Caesar the things that are Caesar's. Paying homage to those who are truly creative, in a discipline often afflicted by amnesia and, alas, all too often associated with the ephemeral – here today, gone tomorrow.

A compass, a marker, allowing us to know what has already been done and redone, and helping us not to do it a third time.

A dialogue between images not intended to be placed side by side. A juxtaposition of two ways of realising the same concept. A conscious or unconscious copy, we soon see that the result is never exactly the same. The differences are in the details.

A kick, an electric shock, a bit of itching powder – all with the intention of raising the creative profession's awareness to certain aspects and getting them to change their ways of working. A form of finger-pointing, getting them to stop acting as if something didn't exist. To get the profession to question its actions, to check the originality of its ideas or at least to give oneself the means to do so. Something which, in 2016, in the era of Internet, online databases and search engines, should not be impossible. Let's be optimistic.

What is originality? Is it actually possible to be 100% original? Hasn't everything already been done? If this is the case, has it all been done in all possible ways? Are we more creative when our heads are completely free of all references to past work? Or on the contrary when we know about everything done in the past? Can we create an idea without any relationship to anything existing? Are we necessarily influenced by the past? And if so, to what extent? Who influences whom? Is it possible to know whether something has already been done? How? Is it necessarily shameful to be treated as a copycat? For whom? Does it call for punishment? What sort of punishment? A child learns by copying its parents. Does the copy have any merits? In what context is a copy acceptable, even desirable? You can't reinvent the wheel. Is that always true? At what level of added value can an idea be considered as renewed rather than plagiarised? **These are just a few of the questions raised by my work. And which are somehow highlighted by this book.**

AVERTISSEMENT AU LECTEUR

Fr

Pas un jour ne passe sans qu'une affaire de plagiat ne fasse le buzz sur les réseaux sociaux. Pas un jour sans qu'on entende en agence de publicité «ça, c'est déjà fait!» «c'est du déjà-vu» ou «ton truc me fait penser à...». Ce sujet est sans cesse au cœur de l'actualité et des préoccupations de tout créatif et ne laisse personne indifférent. La question de l'originalité est une composante essentielle de nos métiers. C'est entre autres pour l'atteindre que l'on paie si cher les talents de certaines agences. Elle contribue de manière significative à différencier les marques, à étonner le public, à sortir du lot et marquer les esprits.

Et pourtant, aussi étrange que cela puisse paraître, un nombre impressionnant de campagnes manque cruellement d'originalité quand elles ne sont pas tout simplement calquées sur d'autres.

Vol? Triche? Manque d'inspiration? Réminiscence inconsciente? Télescopage malheureux? Ma démarche vise avant tout à documenter précisément et à souligner ce curieux phénomène, un peu honteux, souvent caché sous le tapis. Les créatifs se réfugient trop souvent derrière un «c'est pas de chance», «on ne l'a pas fait exprès». J'ai donc voulu une démarche visuelle et coup de poing pour susciter le débat et inciter à la prise de conscience. Afin d'éviter toute mauvaise interprétation de mes intentions, voici quelques points essentiels à connaître avant de vous plonger dans cet ouvrage. En souhaitant que ce livre ne vous serve pas d'inspiration, mais qu'il vous permette de vous poser les bonnes questions avant d'attaquer tout travail de création.

Ce livre n'est pas

Un recueil de pubs «lambda», loin de là. La plupart des créations exposées dans cet ouvrage ont été présentées à de prestigieux festivals de publicité en vue de récompenser leur originalité. Elles ont été vendues cher par des agences qui se revendiquent comme créatives.

Un règlement de comptes. Aucune marque, aucune agence, aucun créatif n'est visé en particulier. On trouve des pubs qui manquent cruellement d'originalité dans tous les pays, et à toutes les époques. Ce livre n'est donc pas une dénonciation calomnieuse ni une attaque ad nominem. Les informations données ne le sont que dans un souci de précision et d'exactitude.

Un jugement de valeur. Jamais je ne prends parti pour dire que l'original est nécessairement meilleur que la redite. L'ensemble des travaux présentés est globalement de très grande qualité. Certains sont juste plus originaux que d'autres, mais les plus aboutis et les plus percutants ne sont pas toujours ceux que l'on croit.

Un ouvrage d'un anti-pub ou autre «casseur de pubs» (*ad-buster*). Je réprouve globalement ces mouvements qui sont avant tout causés – et je le déplore – par un trop-plein de mauvaise publicité. Mon travail est un constat critique et implacable, mais que je souhaite constructif. Il est établi par un passionné d'idées intelligentes, spectaculaires mais avant tout créatives et innovantes. Je suis «masqué» pour me préserver de toute influence et de toute pression. Cette cagoule, c'est aussi un pied de nez aux egos surdimensionnés très courants dans ce métier et qui ne pensent qu'à se montrer.

Un constat global de toutes les sources d'inspiration de la publicité qui sont multiples et variées. Il ne présente aucune campagne qui plagie ou recycle une affiche de cinéma, le travail d'un illustrateur ou une œuvre d'art. Je m'attaque, par choix éditorial, à épingler le plus absurde et le plus grotesque: les pubs qui recyclent des pubs. Bref, le serpent qui se mord la queue.

Une thèse universitaire sur le plagiat ou la réminiscence des idées. Il n'a pas vocation à faire le tour de la question, mais plutôt à l'illustrer de façon percutante et à ouvrir le débat. C'est une preuve par l'image. Je ne cherche pas à justifier, juger ou punir, mais avant tout à informer et à surprendre.

Ce livre est

Un état des lieux, un constat, la photographie d'un phénomène. Je l'ai voulu visuel, facile d'accès et étonnant. Ce constat ne se borne évidemment pas à la publicité imprimée classique. Il s'agit uniquement d'un choix éditorial auquel je me suis soumis afin de viser l'efficacité, de m'adapter le plus possible au support sur lequel il s'inscrit et de traiter de ce que je connais le mieux. Évidemment, on constate aussi un manque d'originalité flagrant dans de nombreuses publicités *online* ou sur mobile, et plus largement dans tout ce qui touche à la création de logotypes, de sites web et aux arts graphiques. Je ne souhaitais pas m'éparpiller.

Le résultat d'une grosse recherche documentaire et iconographique qui a nécessité d'innombrables heures de travail, de collecte et de tri, que ce soit dans des livres, sur des bases de données ou sur le web.

Une invitation à réfléchir: aux questions d'éthique du métier de créatif. Aux méthodes de création et à l'influence de la culture commune. Il soulève de multiples questions et j'en évoque quelques-unes à la fin de cet avant-propos. N'hésitez pas à me faire parvenir les vôtres via les réseaux sociaux.

Une façon ludique de rendre à César ce qui lui appartient. De rendre hommage aux vrais créatifs, dans une discipline souvent frappée d'amnésie et hélas trop souvent liée à l'éphémère, à l'instant présent et à l'oubli.

Une boussole, un repère. Il permet de savoir ce qui a déjà été fait et refait pour ne pas le re-refaire.

Un dialogue entre des images qui n'avaient pas vocation à se côtoyer. Un face-à-face d'une même idée, réalisée de deux manières différentes. Copie consciente ou inconsciente, on se rend compte que le résultat n'est jamais exactement le même. Tout se joue dans les détails.

Un coup de pied, un électrochoc, un poil à gratter destiné à la profession pour l'inciter à une prise de conscience et à modifier cette façon de travailler. Une manière de la pointer du doigt, pour ne plus faire comme si ça n'existait pas. Obliger les créatifs à se remettre en question, à vérifier l'originalité de leurs idées ou tout du moins s'en donner les moyens. Ce qui, en 2016, à l'ère d'internet, des bases de données en ligne et des moteurs de recherche, ne devrait pas être impossible. Soyons optimistes.

Qu'est-ce que l'originalité? Est-il vraiment possible d'être 100% original? Tout a-t-il déjà été fait? Si oui, l'a-t-on fait de toutes les manières? Est-on plus créatif quand on part l'esprit vierge de toute référence? Ou au contraire quand on connaît tout ce qui s'est fait dans le passé? Peut-on engendrer une idée sans parenté? Sommes-nous nécessairement influencés par le passé et à quel degré? Qui influence qui? Est-il possible de savoir si quelque chose a déjà été fait et comment? Est-ce nécessairement une honte d'être traité de copieur? Est-ce grave, et pour qui? Est-ce que cela appelle une punition? De quel ordre? Un enfant apprend bien en copiant sur ses parents. Aussi, la copie possède-t-elle des vertus? Dans quel cadre est-ce acceptable, voire souhaitable? Ce qui est fait n'est plus à refaire. Est-ce toujours vrai? À quel niveau de valeur ajoutée une idée peut-elle être considérée comme renouvelée plutôt que plagiée? **Voilà finalement quelques-unes des questions soulevées par mon travail. Et que ce livre vous pose en filigrane.**

THE MASKED FACE

JÉRÔME RUDONI TALKS TO JOE

En

I've met Joe four times.
The first time, seated in front
of my computer screen in the
early years of this century,
when I switched to studying
advertising. My discovery
of his work helped me become
a copywriter. My second
meeting with this hunter of
copycat ads and defender
of advertising creativity was
less virtual. It was in September
2012, at a conference organised
by his Luxembourg publishing
house to mark the launch of his
second book, *100 visual ideas,
1000 great ads.* We both
wore masks. He was doing
so to maintain his anonymity,
thus enabling him to carry on
acting in complete liberty. I was
doing "ambush marketing",
an action I had dreamed up just
a few hours previously
with the aim of increasing
the visibility of my blog.
The third time was not the best.
This furtive meeting only took
place in my head, when my then
creative director called me in to
his office to tell me the concept
I was thinking about for a major
client was not original at all.
Perhaps even downright copied.
The worst thing was that
I obviously knew about the
original campaign. But had
I just copied it? Possibly.
Unconsciously. I had not seen
him since.

A few years went by, and,
in the meantime, his publishing
house hired me. And now I have
been asked to interview him.
Here's the story of how I got to
meet him for the fourth time.

Hi Joe, I'm not going to kiss your cheek because, between my 3-day beard and your mask, that would be like ripping off Velcro tape. But aren't you getting tired of hiding behind your bank robber mask?

"As the French saying goes, *pour vivre heureux vivons cachés* ('to live happily, you've got to keep your head down'). I won't be telling you anything new when I say that the advertising world is full of people ready to do everything to get in the limelight, to have themselves photographed, featured in magazines. Speaking for myself, I prefer to stay in the background. All those oversized egos are nothing but shit. What counts is how I go about doing things and the questions that it raises, not who I am. Keeping my face masked is thus a way of staying in the background, but also a way of maintaining my freedom to criticise."

Are you saying that there are agencies putting pressure on you?

"It's a small world, and I have been told a number of times that it's not that open to criticism or questioning. I've received insulting emails, I've been called all names under the sun – an informer, a troublemaker, a troll or even a hater as we say today. But things have died down quite a bit since people have started understanding that I'm not targeting anyone in particular. Though I do have something against lazy or ignorant people, and ones who cheat. Strangely enough, nobody seems to see themselves in any of these categories."

Is there at least any trace of creativity in their threats?

"Never. Quite the contrary, they show great creativity in justifying their actions when I catch them red-handed, telling me that they are not to blame, that it's bad luck, that it's the client or the brief at fault…"

Are there any other hunters of copycat ads out there in the world?

"There are a number of more or less well-known blogs and websites on plagiarism, such as *Sounds Just Like[1]* for music or *Culture Samples[2]* on the phenomenon of sampling. In the field of contemporary art and photography, we've got *Part Nouveau[3]* and *Who wore it better[4]*, while there's *Copy Anticopy[5]* for graphic design. But there's no specialised blog for advertising. There are, however, a number of wider-ranging websites such as *Adland* (USA) which have sections on this kind of coincidence. I've seen quite a few blogs appear and disappear over the years, especially websites dedicated to plagiarism in the field of web design and logos. There's a lot of work to be done in this field."

You publish books, give lectures, regularly contribute to specialist magazines. Has "Joe la Pompe" become a full-time job?

"It started off as a game, as a challenge. But over the years it became an increasingly time-consuming hobby. And I did it on top of my work in the advertising agency. But at a certain moment in time, it just got too difficult to work on both fronts due to the sheer amount of work. I hesitated a few years before taking the plunge. For the last 2-3 years,

I've devoted myself 100% to the website. Apart from updating it on a regular basis, this involves many other activities: I work with students (I work as an instructor within the Adprentis network), I cooperate with a number of magazines (*CB News* in France, *Pub* in Belgium, *Cominmag* in Switzerland, *Adformatie* in the Netherlands and *Arab Ad* in Lebanon), and I take part in advertising festivals to make sure they don't give awards to ideas we've already seen (Epica Awards, Les Chatons d'Or…)."

Since I've never seen your face, could it be that our roads have crossed without me even knowing it?

"What with all the various agencies I've been involved within, either working in a creative capacity or presenting my portfolio, all those films and photos I've shot, all those radio recordings I've made… there are hundreds of people I've crossed roads with in the course of my career. So maybe we've met before. I might have been a colleague of yours, your boss or that bastard who didn't like your job. It would seem that in real life I'm much more popular and much less fussy than Joe."

There are obviously people who know who you really are. What do you say to people close to you to prevent them from revealing your identity on Facebook after a night down at the pub?

"Not even my mother recognised me on the cover of my latest book (*100 visual ideas, 1000 great ads*)! And I tell my friends it's all a big joke and that it's much more fun that way. I don't wear a mask because I'm afraid. If someone wants to speak to me or meet me, that can always be arranged… or not. It depends on what he (or she) wants."

But your mother, she must think you're an original. No?

"My mother is an artist, a true one. She makes a living out of her art. And what's more, she doesn't hide behind a pseudonym. Without doubt she instiled in me a certain curiosity as well as a taste for originality and creation. To be quite honest, I resemble quite a lot of people of my generation (the generation X – there's a clue for you). Like me, my persona makes no claim to be unique or inimitable – a great difference to the ads featured in this book: they were all presented as original, innovative and 'firsts' when they came out. To start with, that was false. And even worse, they sought to be rewarded for it. You know, when you have twins in nature, there's nothing you can do about it. But when you give birth to an ad (or any other work, whether artistic or not), you always have the opportunity to check whether it existed beforehand or not."

You defend creativity and originality. At school, were you that kind of kid who covered up his work with his hand to prevent his fellow from copying his work?

"Ahah! What I'm doing now actually developed much later in life. But all of us have 'cheated' at some point in our life. We've all copied from our neighbour, we've all used crib sheets… By the way, I read that Aristotle saw copying as the only real way to learn things, to understand them in order to be capable of creativity. (*Propos sur l'art de la copie*, Éditions L'Art-Dit)."

It's not my business to say whether it's bad or to make any judgement. But I'm quite amused to find that multinational companies' (whether advertising agencies or client companies) creative investments don't match their ambitions. 'Be different', 'Don't imitate, innovate!'... They call themselves original, but don't live up to the expectations. At school, we didn't bother about being original. We just wanted to pass our classes!

You've already said that malevolent people have perhaps visited your website to pick up good ideas and adapt them to their own needs.

"I've heard people say several times that my website is a great source of inspiration. I don't really know whether I should take this as a compliment. If you understand 'adapt them to their own needs' as giving them added value, recycling them in an intelligent manner, then I would agree with this approach.

Do you mean that, as with fashion, something new can be made out of something old?

"Obviously, you're entitled to do so. In fact, that's nearly always what's done. But do we really have to 'do something new'? We no longer invent. All we do is reinvent. Unfortunately, the vast majority of examples in this book don't actually reinvent anything. And that's what I'm denouncing.

At the end of the day, what's better – a good copy or a bad ad?

"Anything's better than a bad ad! But I'm not going to tell you that it's better to be a copycat, even if you're crafty. I could never condone a lazy repeat, even if similar to a very good campaign.

You're always saying that you're not judging, that you're leaving that up to the reader. But the man behind the mask, doesn't he have a deep-rooted opinion?

"I'm not going to severely judge any particular person or agency. But on the other hand I am very critical of the profession as a whole, which permanently gives the impression of reinventing itself (with new digital approaches, augmented reality, big data, the social media) and yet continues to work the same way it has always worked, without doing anything about the problem of copying or the way it can be fought. This problem is being permanently swept under the carpet, side-lined, although, in my opinion, it's a key issue. My book shows the extent of a problem that is affecting everyone.

In the copycat world, is there any country which particularly stands out?

"Generally speaking, it's not so much a matter of country, but rather a lack of experience. The younger the creative people are, the more they lack culture and the more they tend to reuse what already exists. One day, Rémi Babinet (BETC) told me that *'creative people generally have an active memory of about two years'*. Young people belonging to generation Y or Z think they are doing something new just because they're using media that didn't exist a few years ago (Facebook, Twitter, etc.), meanwhile I'm permanently castigating them for recycling jokes and puns that have existed for decades. This generation bottle-fed

on the Internet was called the 'cut and paste' generation in a documentary that I recently saw on TV. These days, it's easier than ever to go onto the web and to make a copy paste.

I've kept the most important question for the end. Since you've been putting your foot down, have you noticed more awareness on the part of creative people? You say that a number of agencies ask you for advice before launching a campaign. That's major. But generally speaking, what's the trend? Are we seeing less copying? Do you think that the advertising profession may one day stop copying? Or are you a Don Quixote fighting against windmills?

"I use to naivly think that, the more my website gained visibility, the fewer examples I would find to castigate. Unfortunately, it's actually quite the oposite. Needless to say that it's an issue. Either everybody's hiding behind a mask, or nobody knows how to remedy the situation. It's probably both. It's a phenomenon which will never completely disappear and a mere blog is not going to put a stop to it. But otherwise my fight is not in vain: the awareness is there, and people have become afraid of getting caught. While it's so easy to copy via the Internet, there'll always be someone on social media making a comment, triggering you to take action. From now on, whether I'm here or not, no copycat can be sure of getting away with it. And that's very different from the days when I started, when whole creative careers could be entirely based on copying without anybody knowing. And that makes me quite optimistic." ∎

1. soundsjustlike.com
2. culture.samples.fr
3. partnouveau.com
4. who-wore-it-better.tumblr.com
5. facebook.com/copy.anticopy

LA FACE CACHÉE

INTERVIEW DE JOE PAR JÉRÔME RUDONI

Fr

J'ai rencontré Joe quatre fois. La première, assis devant mon écran d'ordinateur, début des années 2000, alors que je me réorientais vers des études en publicité. Je découvrais son travail, et il allait sans le savoir orienter le mien, puisque je suis devenu copywriter. La deuxième rencontre avec ce chasseur de publicités jumelles, grand défenseur de la créativité publicitaire, fut moins virtuelle. C'était en septembre 2012, lors d'une conférence organisée par sa maison d'édition au Luxembourg à l'occasion de la sortie de son deuxième livre, *100 visual ideas, 1000 great ads.* Il était cagoulé, moi aussi. Lui, pour garder l'anonymat et continuer à agir librement. Moi, pour une action d'*ambush marketing* imaginée quelques heures plus tôt avec l'objectif

avoué de donner un peu de visibilité à mon blog. La troisième fois ne fut pas la meilleure. Furtive, la rencontre n'a d'ailleurs eu lieu que dans ma tête, au moment où mon directeur de création de l'époque m'avait convoqué pour me dire que le concept que j'avais pondu pour un gros client n'avait rien d'original. Voire même carrément pompé. Le pire, c'est que je connaissais forcément la campagne originale. Mais l'avais-je purement et simplement copiée? Peut-être. Inconsciemment. Je ne l'avais pas revu depuis.

Quelques années sont passées, et entre-temps, sa maison d'édition m'a embauché. Elle me propose aujourd'hui de réaliser son interview. C'est l'histoire de notre quatrième rencontre.

Salut Joe, je ne te fais pas la bise parce qu'entre ma barbe de trois jours et la laine de ta cagoule, ça va faire effet velcro. D'ailleurs, t'en as pas marre de te cacher sous ton masque de braqueur de banque?

«Pour vivre heureux vivons cachés (*citation pompée, ndlr*). Je ne t'apprendrais rien en te disant que le monde de la publicité est rempli de gens qui sont prêts à tout pour se faire voir, se faire photographier, faire la une des magazines, alors ça me plaît d'être discret et à contre-courant! Merde aux égos surdimensionnés. Ce qui compte, c'est ma démarche et les questions qu'elle pose, non pas qui je suis. Si j'agis face cachée, c'est donc une manière de rester en retrait, mais c'est aussi pour préserver ma liberté critique.

Tu veux dire qu'il y a des agences qui te mettent la pression?

«C'est un petit monde, et on m'a souvent fait comprendre qu'il n'était pas très ouvert à la critique ni à la remise en question. J'ai reçu des mails d'insulte, on m'a traité de tout, de délateur, de fouteur de merde, d'empêcheur de tourner en rond, de *troll* ou encore de *hater* comme on dit aujourd'hui. Ça s'est quand même bien calmé depuis que tout le monde a compris que je n'en voulais à personne 'en particulier'. J'en veux juste aux paresseux, aux incultes et aux tricheurs. Mais bizarrement, personne ne se reconnaît jamais dans aucune de ces catégories.

Est-ce qu'au moins ils font preuve de créativité dans leurs menaces?

«Jamais. Par contre, ils font preuve de beaucoup de créativité dans leurs justifications une fois que je les prends la main dans le sac, pour m'expliquer qu'ils n'y sont pour rien, que c'est la faute à pas de chance, au client, au brief...

Existe-t-il d'autres chasseurs de publicités jumelles dans le monde?

«Il existe d'autres blogs et sites connus ou moins connus sur la thématique du plagiat, notamment dans la musique comme *Sounds Just Like*[1] ou *Culture Samples*[2] sur le phénomène du sampling; dans le domaine de l'art contemporain et de la photo, il y a *Part Nouveau*[3] et *Who wore it better*[4]; *Copy Anticopy*[5] dans le domaine du design graphique, mais dans le domaine de la publicité, il n'y a pas d'autre blog dédié. Certains sites comme *Adland* (USA) ont cependant des rubriques qui relayent aussi ce genre de coïncidences, mais n'en font pas leur sujet unique. J'ai vu plusieurs blogs se créer et disparaître au fil des années, notamment des sites dédiés au plagiat dans le domaine du webdesign et des logos. Là aussi, il y a du boulot...

Tu publies des livres, tu donnes des conférences, tu as des contributions régulières dans différents magazines spécialisés... «Joe la Pompe», c'est devenu un métier à plein temps?

«Ça a commencé comme un jeu, comme un défi, et puis au fur et à mesure des années, c'est devenu un hobby de plus en plus chronophage. Je faisais ça en plus, à côté de mes heures de travail en agence de publicité. Mais à un moment donné, ça a été de plus en plus difficile de mener les deux de front étant donné la masse de travail à gérer. J'ai hésité pendant quelques années et puis j'ai dû faire un choix. Depuis deux-trois ans, j'ai décidé de me lancer et de me consacrer à 100% au site. Ça se traduit par de multiples activités au-delà de sa mise à jour régulière: je fais des interventions devant des étudiants (je suis formateur au sein du collectif Adprentis), je collabore à des magazines (*CB News* en France, *Pub* en Belgique, *Cominmag* en Suisse, *Adformatie* aux Pays-Bas et *Arab Ad* au Liban) et je participe à des festivals publicitaires pour faire en sorte qu'ils ne priment pas des idées déjà vues (Epica Awards, Les Chatons d'Or...).

Vu que je n'ai jamais vu ton visage, si ça se trouve je te côtoie dans la vie et je ne le sais même pas?

«Entre les différentes agences dans lesquelles je suis passé en tant que créatif et celles où j'ai présenté mon portfolio, les films que j'ai tournés, les photos que j'ai shootées, les enregistrements de radio que j'ai menés... j'ai rencontré des centaines de personnes dans ma carrière, donc oui, on s'est peut-être déjà croisé. J'ai peut-être été ton collègue, ton chef ou l'enfoiré qui n'a pas aimé ton dossier. Il paraît que dans la vie, je suis beaucoup plus sympa et beaucoup moins pointilleux que Joe.

Il y a forcément des gens qui connaissent ta double identité. Tu dis quoi aux personnes de ton entourage pour qu'elles ne te balancent pas publiquement sur Facebook à chaque soirée arrosée?

«Ma mère ne m'a pas reconnu sur la couverture de mon dernier livre (*100 visual ideas, 1000 great ads, ndlr*), c'est pour te dire! Sinon, à mes amis, je leur dis que tout ça est une blague et que c'est beaucoup plus marrant ainsi. Je ne me cache pas par peur, si quelqu'un veut me parler ou me rencontrer, il y a toujours moyen de s'arranger... ou pas. Ça dépend de ce qu'il (ou elle) veut.

Ta mère justement, elle doit te prendre pour un original, non?

«Ma mère, c'est une artiste, une vraie. Elle vit de son art. Et en plus elle ne se cache pas derrière un pseudonyme... Sans doute m'a-t-elle inculqué en même temps qu'une certaine curiosité le goût de l'originalité et de la création. La vérité, c'est que je ressemble à beaucoup de gens de ma génération (la génération X, voilà je te balance un indice). Comme moi, mon personnage n'a pas la prétention d'être unique ou inimitable, à la différence des publicités qui sont épinglées dans ce livre: elles se sont toutes présentées comme originales, innovantes et 'jamais vues' au moment de leur sortie. D'abord c'est faux, et le pire, c'est qu'elles ont cherché à se faire récompenser pour ça! Tu sais, quand on a un jumeau dans la nature, on n'y peut rien. Par contre, quand on donne naissance à une publicité (ou à n'importe quelle œuvre, artistique ou non), on a toujours la possibilité de vérifier qu'elle n'a pas déjà été faite avant.

Tu défends la créativité, l'originalité. À l'école, t'étais du genre à cacher ta copie avec ta main pour que tes camarades ne s'inspirent pas de tes réponses?

«Ah ah! Ça m'est venu beaucoup plus tard en réalité. On a tous 'triché' dans nos vies à un moment ou un autre. On a tous copié sur le voisin, pratiqué les antisèches… Par ailleurs, j'ai lu que Aristote considérait la copie comme étant la seule bonne manière d'apprendre les choses, de les comprendre pour pouvoir être créatif (*Propos sur l'art de la copie*, Éditions L'Art-Dit). Je ne suis pas là pour dire que c'est mal ou pour juger. Je m'amuse juste dans ma démarche à constater que des multinationales (agences de pub comme annonceurs) ne se donnent pas les moyens de leurs ambitions créatives. 'Be different', 'n'imitez pas, innovez!'… Ils s'autoproclament originaux et ne le sont pas forcément. À l'école, on s'en foutait d'être originaux, on voulait surtout avoir la moyenne!

Tu t'es déjà dit que peut-être, il y avait des gens malintentionnés qui venaient sur ton site pour piquer des bonnes idées et les refaire à leur sauce?
«J'ai entendu plusieurs fois des gens dire que mon site était une formidable source d'inspiration. Je ne sais pas comment prendre ce compliment. Maintenant si par 'refaire à leur sauce' tu entends y amener de la valeur ajoutée, recycler intelligemment, améliorer, alors là oui je suis d'accord!

Comme dans la mode, on aurait donc le droit de refaire du neuf avec du vieux?
«On a le droit, bien sûr. D'ailleurs on ne fait presque que ça. Mais encore faut-il vraiment 'faire du neuf'. On n'invente plus, on réinvente. Malheureusement, la très grande majorité des exemples exposés dans ce livre ne réinvente rien du tout, c'est ce que je dénonce.

Au fond, c'est mieux quoi, une bonne pompe ou une mauvaise publicité?
«Tout vaut mieux qu'une mauvaise pub! Mais tu ne me feras pas dire pour autant qu'il faut pomper, même si tu es rusé. Une reprise paresseuse et à l'identique même d'une très bonne campagne, ça, je ne pourrai jamais le cautionner.

Tu dis partout que tu ne portes pas de jugement, que tu laisses le lecteur se faire le sien. Mais l'homme sous la cagoule, il a forcément un avis tranché?
«Je n'ai pas un jugement sévère sur une personne ou une agence en particulier, mais par contre je suis très critique envers la profession dans son ensemble qui fait mine de se réinventer en permanence (avec le digital, la réalité augmentée, le *big data*, le *social media*) et qui par derrière continue d'agir de la même façon depuis des dizaines d'années sans rien changer sur la problématique du plagiat et la manière d'y faire face ou d'y remédier. Ce problème est caché sous le tapis, minimisé et marginalisé en permanence alors que je pense qu'il est central. Mon travail montre bien l'étendue du problème qui n'épargne personne.

Dans le monde de la pompe, y a-t-il un pays qui se démarque particulièrement?
«D'une manière générale, ce n'est pas tellement une question de pays, mais plutôt de manque d'expérience. Plus les créatifs sont jeunes, plus ils manquent de culture et plus ils ont tendance à refaire ce qui existe déjà. Un jour, Rémi Babinet (BETC) m'a confié qu''*en général, les créatifs ont une mémoire

vive de deux ans'. Les jeunes de la génération Y ou Z pensent faire du nouveau juste parce qu'ils utilisent des médias qui n'existaient pas quelques années plus tôt (Facebook, Twitter…), alors que je les épingle en permanence à recycler des blagues et des jeux de mots éculés depuis des décennies. Cette génération biberonnée à internet a d'ailleurs été appelée la génération 'copier-coller' dans un reportage que j'ai vu récemment à la TV. Aujourd'hui, il est plus facile que jamais d'aller sur le web et d'y faire un Pomme+C Pomme+V.

J'ai gardé la question la plus importante pour la fin. Est-ce que depuis que tu sévis, tu as senti une prise de conscience de la part des créatifs? Tu dis que certaines agences te consultent avant de lancer une campagne. C'est fort. Mais globalement, quelle est la tendance? Est-ce qu'on pompe moins? Penses-tu qu'un jour la publicité ne copiera plus la publicité? Ou au contraire, ton combat est-il vain?
«Je pensais innocemment que plus mon site serait connu, moins je trouverais d'exemples à épingler dessus, et je dois avouer que c'est plutôt le contraire. Il y a donc un souci. Soit tout le monde se voile la face, soit personne ne sait comment y remédier. Sans doute les deux. C'est un phénomène qui ne disparaîtra jamais complètement et il n'est pas du pouvoir d'un blog de l'endiguer, mais pour autant, mon combat n'est pas vain: la prise de conscience et la peur d'être épinglé sont devenues réelles. Sur internet, on copie facilement, mais il y aura toujours quelqu'un sur les réseaux sociaux, au détour d'un commentaire, pour vous ressortir vos casseroles. Désormais, que je sois là ou pas, personne ne peut copier en étant certain d'être épargné. Ce qui est un énorme changement par rapport au moment où j'ai commencé, et où des carrières entières de créatifs se sont faites grâce au plagiat 'ni vu ni connu' qui ne ressortait jamais. C'est ce qui me rend optimiste.» ■

1. soundsjustlike.com
2. culture.samples.fr
3. partnouveau.com
4. who-wore-it-better.tumblr.com
5. facebook.com/copy.anticopy

WHY SO MANY SIMILAR IDEAS?

En

When busted trying to rip off an idea, people tend to have an infinite number of justifications as to why it happened. Regardless of that, shedding light on some of the major ones seemed important to me.

Quite simply because **two people can have the same idea** (including at the same time), in the knowledge that thousands of brains are working on the same problems all over the world.

Because **there are cheats.** In France, advertisers tend to have a bad reputation (scarcely better than that of second-hand car salesmen or traffic wardens) and no professional environment exists that is 100% honest. This is still a marginal explanation, but nevertheless real. Dishonesty can be spurred on by the pressure on creative minds, especially at times of crisis.

In an agency, the **briefs are often the same.** The creation processes are more or less identical on every continent. **Culture has become globalised** and the same references are to be found everywhere. What is more, advertisers tend to be followers rather than trendsetters or originators of fashion. They proceed to a large extent through recovery, recycling, misappropriation and adaptation.

It is possible in certain cases that it is a **client requirement.** The advertisers often have as their benchmark the campaigns (or products) of their competitors and, for fear of taking risks, are rather inclined to imitate them. Normally speaking, it is the role of the agency to dissuade them from doing so. But who wants to fall out with a client?

All the creative schemes, all the persuasive techniques have already been explored since the Mad Men era. Millions of publicity campaigns have already been created which all use one of these ingredients (provocation, seduction, devil's advocate, parody, exaggeration, etc.), it is therefore very hard today to restate without repeating.

The world's creative minds use the same equipment (Apple), the same applications (Photoshop, InDesign, etc.) and visit the same sites for inspiration: Ads of the World, Cannes Archive, Fubiz, Getty Images, Fotolia, etc.

The prizes for creativity, such as the Cannes Lions, have become increasingly important for the creative minds and the agencies. This means that **people will do anything to win one of these trophies** (including cheating, sucking up and recycling). Moreover, since the adverts are judged by international panels, they have to be rapidly comprehensible to everyone, which leads to an inevitable standardisation in the form of content submitted.

An incredible general speeding up of deadlines has occurred in recent years. Whereas some thirty years ago, several months were given in which to design and deliver a campaign, these deadlines have been shortened to a few weeks, then to a few days in recent years, when it is not "real-time" work which is required. Under these conditions, **there is no time to check whether an idea already exists.** Still less to start again if it is realised that this is the case. And even if there is time to check, no one is inclined or has the required skills to set about doing so.

In a world of ever-tighter constraints (particularly relating to budgetary and legal matters), the originality of a campaign is generally considered, regrettably in my view, as an additional constraint, the icing on the cake or simply a creative whim when it is actually at the heart of an agency's added value and should be considered as a real priority.

A large number of advertisers unfortunately show evidence of **intellectual laziness.** One of the shortcomings that has struck me the most is the very human habit of stopping at the first good idea encountered. You can bet your bottom dollar that something will almost certainly be produced that already exists.

How to avoid these unwanted situations?

Regardless of the subject, even if you are not copying and believe that you have created your own idea without any direct inspiration, **you should always consider that others could have had the same idea before you.**

Thousands of pieces of information and advertising messages are ingested daily. Our brains are continually bombarded with stimuli. Creative minds keep a sharp eye open and, to get their bearings, observe the work of others very closely. This leads to a **risk of subconscious reminiscing,** otherwise known as cryptomnesia (see glossary).

You will always save time by checking that an idea does not already exist rather than starting again from scratch after a film has been made or a photo taken. Giving birth to an idea can take months in terms of advertising, whereas research rarely takes more than a few hours.

The average age of the creative minds in an advertising agency is very low (25-35 years). General amnesia reigns there and **there are few genuine creative older staff who can stand back and have a good advertising culture.** In France, unfortunately, experience is little valued and a creative mind which is too old is wrongly too quickly seen as a "has been".

In case of doubt or time constraints or if researching existing ideas seems too complicated, ask Joe for his opinion!

joelapompe.net/services

POURQUOI TANT D'IDÉES SIMILAIRES?

Il existe autant de raisons que de justifications données par ceux qui se font prendre la main dans le sac de recycler de vieilles idées, c'est-à-dire un nombre infini. Néanmoins, il me semblait important de faire un point sur les principales.

Tout simplement parce que **deux personnes peuvent avoir la même idée** (y compris au même moment), sachant que des milliers de cerveaux planchent sur les mêmes problématiques aux quatre coins du monde.

Parce qu'**il y a des tricheurs.** En France, les publicitaires ont plutôt mauvaise réputation (à peine meilleure que celle des garagistes ou des fouriéristes), et qu'il n'existe aucun milieu professionnel 100% honnête. Ça reste une explication marginale, mais néanmoins réelle. La malhonnêteté peut être encouragée par la pression subie par les créatifs, notamment en période de crise.

En agence, **les briefs sont souvent les mêmes.** Les process de création sont plus ou moins identiques sur tous les continents. **La culture s'est mondialisée** et les mêmes références se retrouvent partout. De plus, les publicitaires sont plus des suiveurs que des initiateurs de tendances ou de modes. Ils procèdent beaucoup par récupération, recyclage, détournement, adaptation.

Il se peut que ce soit dans certains cas **une demande du client.** Les annonceurs ont souvent comme référence les campagnes (ou les produits) de leurs concurrents et par peur de prendre des risques sont assez enclins à les imiter. Normalement, c'est le rôle de l'agence de les en dissuader. Mais qui a envie de se fâcher avec son client?

Les créatifs du monde entier utilisent le même matériel (Apple), les mêmes applications (Photoshop, InDesign...) et vont sur les mêmes sites d'inspiration: Ads of the World, Cannes Archive, Fubiz, Getty Images, Fotolia...

Tous les schémas créatifs, toutes les techniques de persuasion ont déjà été explorés depuis l'époque des Mad Men. Des millions de campagnes de pub ont déjà été créées qui utilisent toutes l'un de ces ingrédients (la provocation, la séduction, le contre-pied, la parodie, l'exagération...), il est donc très dur aujourd'hui de se redire sans se répéter.

Les prix créatifs tels que les Cannes Lions ont pris de plus en plus d'importance pour les créatifs et pour les agences. Ce qui fait que **les gens sont prêts à tout pour décrocher un de ces trophées** (y compris à tricher, pomper, recycler). Par ailleurs, les pubs étant jugées par des jurys internationaux, elles se doivent d'être compréhensibles rapidement par tout le monde, d'où une inévitable uniformisation dans la forme des contenus qui y sont soumis.

On constate ces dernières années une incroyable accélération généralisée des délais. Alors qu'il y a une trentaine d'années on avait plusieurs mois pour concevoir et livrer une campagne, ces délais se sont raccourcis à quelques semaines puis à quelques jours ces dernières années, quand ce n'est pas un travail en «real-time» qui est demandé. Dans ces conditions, **on n'a pas le temps de vérifier si une idée existe déjà.** Encore moins de tout recommencer si on se rend compte que c'est le cas. Et quand bien même on aurait le temps de vérifier, personne n'a envie de s'y coller ni n'a les compétences requises pour le faire.

Dans un monde de contraintes de plus en plus fortes (notamment budgétaires ou encore juridiques), l'originalité d'une campagne est plus souvent vue, et je le déplore, comme une contrainte de plus, une cerise sur le gâteau, voire une simple lubie de créatifs. Alors même que c'est au cœur de la valeur ajoutée d'une agence et que ça devrait être une vraie priorité.

De nombreux publicitaires font hélas preuve de **paresse intellectuelle.** Un des travers que j'ai le plus constaté par moi-même est cette manie – très humaine au demeurant – de s'arrêter à la première bonne idée trouvée. C'est l'assurance quasi certaine de produire quelque chose qui existe déjà.

Comment éviter ça?

Quel que soit le sujet, même si vous ne copiez pas et que vous pensez avoir créé une idée qui vous est propre et libre de toute inspiration directe, **dites-vous toujours que d'autres ont pu avoir la même idée avant vous.**

On ingère quotidiennement des milliers d'informations et de messages publicitaires. Notre cerveau est bombardé continuellement de stimuli. Les créatifs font beaucoup de veille et pour se faire l'œil observent beaucoup les travaux des autres. D'où **un risque de réminiscence inconsciente,** autrement appelé cryptomnésie (voir lexique).

Vous perdrez toujours moins de temps à vérifier qu'une idée n'a pas déjà été faite qu'à tout recommencer de zéro une fois un film réalisé ou une photo shootée. Accoucher d'une idée peut prendre des mois en publicité, une recherche vous prend rarement plus de quelques heures.

L'âge moyen des créatifs en agence de pub est très bas (25-35 ans). Il y règne une amnésie généralisée et **il y a peu de vrais créatifs séniors qui ont du recul et une bonne culture publicitaire.** En France, hélas, l'expérience est peu valorisée, et un créatif trop vieux est à tort trop vite perçu comme «has been».

En cas de doute, de manque de temps ou si la recherche d'antériorité vous paraît trop complexe... demandez son avis à Joe!

joelapompe.net/services

THE GALLERY

En

This book is interactive:
***Copy Paste* presents 618 ad campaigns,**
but only 247 original advertising concepts.
Coincidence or copycat? Be the judge!
   A tag was assigned to each concept.
If the #hashtag is green, Joe invites you to
take a stand, by giving your opinion online:

→ Visit *www.joelapompe.net*
→ In the search engine, enter the #hashtag
→ Coincidence or copycat? Find out within a click.

LA GALERIE

Fr

Ce livre est interactif:
Copy Paste présente 618 campagnes,
mais seulement 247 concepts publicitaires.
Alors, coïncidence ou copycat? *Be the judge*!
    À chacun des concepts a été attribué un mot-clé.
Lorsque le #hashtag est vert, Joe vous invite à
prendre position, en donnant votre avis en ligne:

→ Rendez-vous sur *www.joelapompe.net*
→ Dans la barre de recherche, entrez le #hashtag
→ Coïncidence ou copycat? Jugez en un clic.

2009

#smelly-dog

2007

2007
South Africa. ***Breath mints for dogs*** by DraftFCB Johannesburg *for YipYap*

2009
Germany. ***Bad dog breath?*** by Publicis Frankfurt *for Tetra 8in1 Dental Snacks*

2008

#strong-nails

2006

2006
Sweden. ***Nutritional supplement for nails*** by Ogilvy & Mather *for Friggs Nutri Cosmetics*

2008
Austria. ***For extra strong, extra long nails*** by TBWA Vienna *for Nivea Calcium Power*

2009

#garfield

PANTONE® 158 C

There can only be one.

2014

2009

Mexico. *We match any color* by RT&A Monterrey *for Comex Paints*

2014

China. *There can only be one* by Young & Rubicam Shanghai *for Pantone*

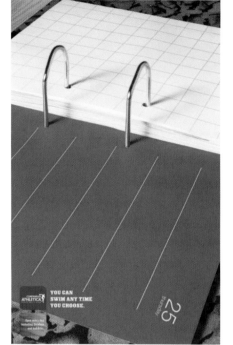

2005

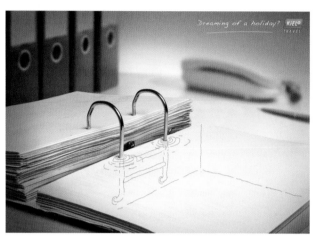

#paper-pool

2012

2002

2002
The Philippines. By TBWA
for Shangri-La

2005
Brazil. By DDB
for Companhia Athletica

2012
Serbia. By New Moment,
New Ideas Young
& Rubicam *for Kielo Travel*

#global-cooling

1998

2001

1998
United Kingdom. By DLKW
Lowe London *for Labatt
Ice Beer*

2001
France. By Ogilvy &
Mather Paris *for
Perrier sparkling water*

2006

#embarrassing-situation

2008

2006

Canada. *You fart 14 times
a day. We can explain* by
Rethink *for Science World*

2008

Venezuela. By Leo Burnett
for Anti-Gas Antifom 40

2001

2009

2001

Brazil. By Ogilvy & Mather
for Matchbox Toys

2009

United States.
By TunnelBravo Mesa
(Arizona) *for HobbyTown
USA*

For a child, this is how a car looks like in the street.
Respect speed limits.

Attitudes
A social initiative by Audi.

Audi
Vorsprung durch Technik

2011

#behind-windbags

To kids the road looks different.
Parents of Child Road Victims

2007

2007

Belgium. *To kids the
road looks different*
by Happiness Brussels
*for OVK Parents
of Child Road Victims*

2011

Spain. By DDB Barcelona
for Audi / Road Prevention

2000

dangerous-slope

2004-A

2009

2004-B

2000

Canada. By BBDO
for Jeep Cherokee

2004-A

Brazil. By Artplan Rio de
Janeiro *for Peugeot*

2004-B

Germany. By Grabarz &
Partner Werbeagentur
for Volkswagen Touareg

2009

Russia. By DDB
for Volkswagen Touareg

2009

#deflated

2009

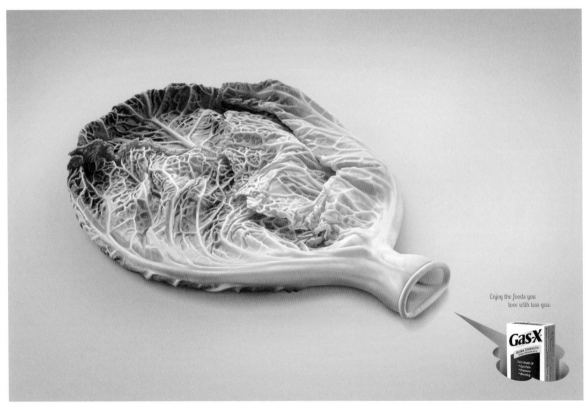

Enjoy the foods you
love with less gas.

2014

2009
India. By Ogilvy &
Mather Gurgaon for
ENO Digestive Tablets

2014
Canada. ***Enjoy the foods you
love with less gas*** by Saatchi
& Saatchi Toronto *for Gas-X*

faster-than-fast

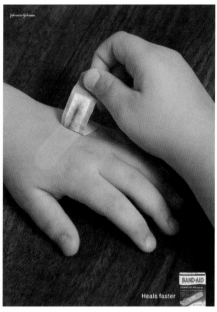

2009-A

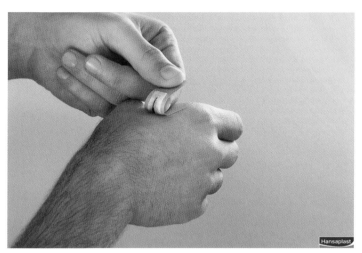

2009-B

2009-A
UAE. By JWT Dubai
for Band-Aid

2009-B
UAE. By TBWA/RAAD Dubai
for Hansaplast

#flame-grilled

2005

2008

2005
Germany. By Ogilvy &
Mather Frankfurt
for Kraft Mexican Ketchup

2008
Turkey. By Lowe
for Calve Hot Ketchup

2001

mud-mask

2007

2001
Brazil. **Stay young**
by FCB *for Jeep*

2007
Argentina. **Mud Therapy**
by FCB Buenos Aires *for Jeep*

2007

#washing-wheels

2008

2007
South Korea. By Cheil
Worldwide *for Samsung
Washing Machines*

2008
Israel. **Keeps on working**
by GPS Advertising Tel Aviv
*for Constructa
Washing Machines*

ONTDEK HOE GOED
JE GRIJSGEDRAAIDE
IDOLEN NOG KLINKEN

2011

ROCK LIVES
JULY 13
INTERNATIONAL
DAY OF ROCK

n

Ipanema 94.9 FM

2013

IT'S A WHOLE DIFFERENT STORY.

FORCE ONE
BLINDADOS
www.forceoneblindados.com.br

2014-A

SBi

2014-B

2011
The Netherlands.
Discover just how great your old heroes still sound by Doorn & Ross for The Mega Record & CD Fair

2013
Brazil. By Dez Comunicação Porto Alegre *for Ipanema Radio FM*

2014-A
Brazil. *It's a whole different story* by Artplan *for Force One Security*

2014-B
Brazil. By Propeg *for SBI Armored Cars*

2011

2011

#tiredness

Do it on the Bus

Do more while you get around ➤➤ **Metro**Transit

doitonthebus.ca

New Rides. Better Service.

2013

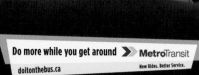

Do it on the Bus

Do more while you get around ➤➤ **Metro**Transit

doitonthebus.ca

New Rides. Better Service.

2013

2011
Sweden. By King Stockholm
for Swedish Rail SJ

2013
Canada. By Acart Com
Ottawa *for Halifax Bus
Metro Transit*

dead-cold

MAYBE EMERGENCY TRAINING IS FOR YOU.   fire-etc.ca
A division of Lakeland College

2007

save the mountain
PARTICIPATE IN OUR CLEAN THE SLOPES DAYS
mountain
riders

more info on mountain-riders.org

2012

2007
Canada. *Maybe emergency training is for you* by Calder Bateman Edmonton *for Fire-etc Emergency Training School*

2012
France. *Save the mountain* by Marcel Paris *for Mountain Riders*

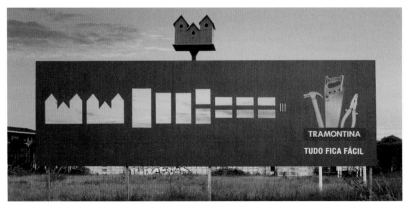

#birdhouse

2010-A

2010-A
Canada. *Hardware made easy* by LG2 Montreal (Québec) *for Canac*

2010-B

2010-B
Brazil. *Build it easily* by DCS Porto Alegre *for Tramontina*

SUR LA ROUTE, CHANGEZ DE COMPORTEMENT AVANT QU'IL NE SOIT TROP TARD.

SÉCURITÉ ROUTIÈRE TOUS RESPONSABLES

2008

#farewell

Saki **roule vite mort pli vite!**

2013

2008
Republic of Mauritius.
By P&P Link *for Road Safety of Mauritius Island*

2013
France (La Réunion).
By Facto Saatchi & Saatchi *for Road Safety*

#tattooed-babies

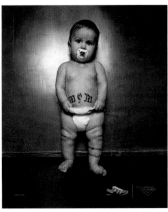

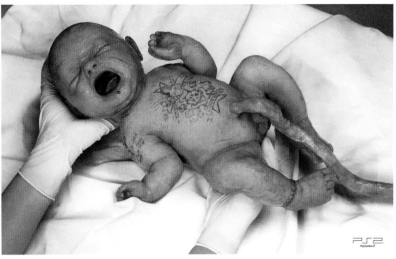

2004

2006

NINGUÉM QUER VER O SEU BEBÉ PRESO

2012

For difficult little people.

2013

2004
United States. By Goodby Silverstein & Partners San Francisco *for Pony*

2006
France. By TBWA Paris *for Sony Playstation 2*

2012
Portugal. By Lintas *for Microlax baby*

2013
United States. By Grey Healthy *for Playtex Baby*

2008-A

2008-A

2008-A

expensive-origamis

SEND AND RECEIVE MONEY FROM COLOMBIA
TO THE MIDDLE EAST OR ANYWHERE IN THE WORLD.

INTERNATIONAL DRAFTS

DAVIVIENDA
BANK

2008-B

SEND AND RECEIVE MONEY FROM COLOMBIA
TO RUSSIA OR ANYWHERE IN THE WORLD.

INTERNATIONAL DRAFTS

DAVIVIENDA
BANK

2008-B

2010

2010

2008-A

Brazil. By Fischer America São Paulo *for Valor Economico Newspaper*

2008-B

Colombia. **Send and receive money from Colombia to the Middle East...** by Leo Burnett Bogota *for Davivienda Bank / Money Transfer*

2010

Spain. **It gets wherever it has to** by Zapping M&C Saatchi Madrid *for Western Union / Money Transfer*

2006

2010

ALWAYS DISCOUNT FOR STUDENTS.

2011

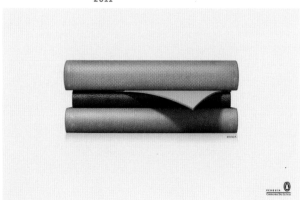

2015

2006	**2010**	**2011**	**2015**
Sweden. By DDB Stockholm *for McDonald's*	Egypt. By DDB Cairo *for Mo'men*	Sweden. *Always discount for students* by Shout Advertising *for Burger King*	Brazil. *Devour* by Young & Rubicam São Paulo *for Penguin Books*

big-splash

2013-A

2013-B

2013-A
France. By Marcel Paris
for Samsung Galaxy Mega

2013-B
Vietnam.
By Ogilvy & Mather
for Megastar Cineplex

2012-A

#continental-drift

2012-B

2012-A
Turkey. By DDB & Co
Istanbul *for Wildlife
Preservation Organization*

2012-B
Russia. *We are one*
by BBDO Moscow *for WWF*

#turnaround

2004

2011

2004
Canada. By DDB
for Energizer Batteries

2011
United States. *Lasts longer*
by Fischer America
for Rayovac Batteries

#shut-up

2014

2015

2014
Guatemala. *Noise
canceling headphones*
by Ogilvy & Mather
for Harman Kardon

2015
Turkey. *Noise
canceling headphones*
by Rafineri Istanbul
for Polk Audio / CAN Hi-Fi

2005

2005

#personal-jewellery

Because hair is your most beautiful accessory: Iam Haircare.

2011

2011

2005
Japan. *Gentle hair care products* by Beacon Communications Tokyo for Wella (Procter & Gamble)

2011
Switzerland. *I am professional haircare* by Young & Rubicam Zurich for Migros

MOYA
MUSEUM OF YOUNG ART

warhol-family

2007

Artists born here.

CIVITA ART SCH
www.civita.it

2011

BORNTODOTHIS.COM
JOHN CASABLANCAS INTERNATIONAL INSTITUTE

JCI INSTITUTE

2012

2007
Austria. By Publicis
*for MOYA, Museum
of young arts*

2011
Italy. **Artists born here**
by Yes I Am Roma
for Civita Art School

2012
Canada. By Spring
Vancouver *for JCI Institute*

#bones

2010

2009

2009

India. **Strong Bones** by
Saatchi & Saatchi Mumbai
for Sandoz Novartis Calcium

2010

Indonesia. By Publicis
Jakarta *for Dumocalcin
Actavis Calcium Tablets*

2008-B

acting-school

2008-A

2008-A

United States. By Hoopafied
for School of acting

2008-B

Bolivia. By BBDO *for Escuela
de Cine y Artes Audiovisuales*

#time-bomb

2010

2014

2010
Jordan. *Beware the risk
of counterfeit parts*
by Tamer Tayyan *for Nissan*

2014
Brazil. *Always use original
parts* by Havas Worldwide
for Citroën

big-splash

2009

2014

2009
Belgium. *Fashion for walls*
by TBWA Brussels
for Levis Paints

2014
France. By Toy *for Les
Décoratives, Paillett' Paints*

2005

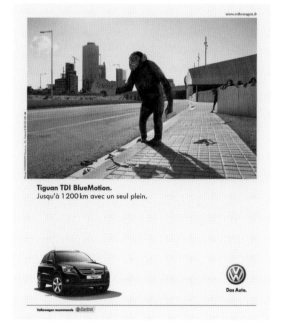

Tiguan TDI BlueMotion.
Jusqu'à 1 200 km avec un seul plein.

2010

THE ALL NEW DEFENDER

2008

2005
United States. By M&C
Saatchi Los Angeles *for
San Diego Zoo*

2008
UAE. By Young & Rubicam
Dubai *for Land Rover
Defender*

2010
France. By Agence V
*for Volkswagen Tiguan
Blue Motion*

2000

2011

furry-sofa

2015

2000
France. By Grey Paris
for *Fébrèze*

2011
Russia. **Oh, so pretty!**
by Power CS Novokuznetsk
for *Alto Furniture*

2015
Chile. **For cats that
don't move much**
by Porta Santiago for
Champion Katt Petfood

double-ejaculation

BOILING HORMONES

Celebrating the agency 15th anniversary, Jump! created a two-page ad in which the pages were glued together using tiny pieces of two-sided adhesive tape, to bring an even more literal and humorous effect to the image. Whenever opening the magazine, the reader would have to unstick both pages, as if finding a 15-year-old boy "damaged" erotic magazine. The ad was published in a brazilian advertising yearbook.

2010

2007

2007
Argentina. *Men's Magazine* by Leo Burnett Buenos Aires *for Humo Magazine*

2010
Brazil. *Boiling hormones for 15 years* by Jump! Comunicação Maringá (Paraná) *for Jump!*

#ashamed

2013

2006

2006
The Philippines. By Ogilvy & Mather *for Pond's Facial Wash*

2013
Israel. By McCann Erickson Tel Aviv *for Dove*

"Bana bir şey olmaz"
deme, okey mi?

O.K.

www.ok.com.tr

2009

dangerous

LEARNED HOW
TO TAKE RISKS
WITH HIS DAD.
STARTED SMOKING AT HOME

SMOKING IS THE LEADING CAUSE OF
MANY KINDS OF DEATHS YOU CAN AVOID
MAY 31. WORLD NO TOBACCO DAY

centralclinic
Specialized Cancer
Treatment Center

2013-A

It's even riskier to
keep ignoring his
high LDL-C.

Add EZETROL

2013-B

2009
Turkey. **Don't say,
"It won't happen to me"**
by RPM Radar Istanbul
for OK Condoms

2013-A
Brazil. **Learned how to
take risks with his dad.
Started smoking at home**
by Brancozulu São Paulo
*for Central Clinic
Cancer Treatment*

2013-B
New Zealand. **It's even
riskier to keep ignoring
his high LDL-C** by BCG2
Auckland *for Ezetrol
(against heart-attacks)*

2006

2011

fly-away

2014

2007

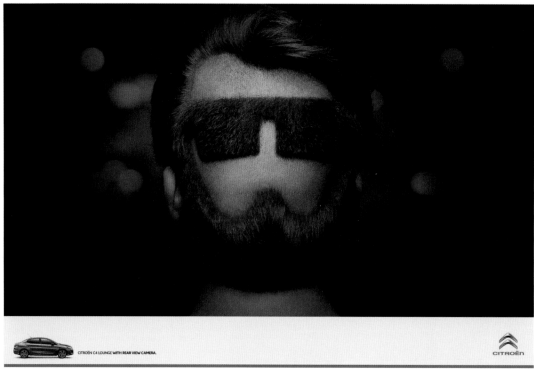

rearview

2014-A

2014-B

2007
Canada. By BleuBlancRouge
for Orbite Hair Salon

2014-A
Brazil. ***With rear view
camera*** by Havas São Paulo
for Citroën C4

2014-B
Germany. By Jung von Matt
*for Mercedes-Benz
360° camera*

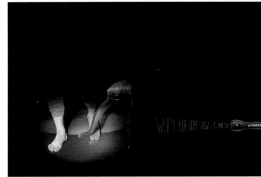

2013

2009

DON'T TRUST THE DARK
360 DEGREE LIGHTING

Energizer.

2009
South Africa. **Don't trust the dark** by DDB Johannesburg *for Energizer*

2013
Romania. **When your home shows its dark side** by Publicis Bucharest *for Varta*

shaved-ice

2008-A

2008-B

2008-A
Australia. By JWT Sydney *for Schick Quattro*

2008-B
United States. By BBDO New York *for Gillette Fusion*

NOW SERVING SALADS

2003

FRESH & Tasty

DALLAS FARMERS MARKET

2013

2015-A

SIEMENS

BAKED ASPARAGUS MARINATED IN WHITE TRUFFLE OIL AND LEMON JUICE SERVED WITH CHAMPAGNE WINE VINEGAR

COOK
SLOW FOOD,
FAST.

2015-B

SUPREME
COUNCIL OF HEALTH

CHOOSE HEALTHY EATING HABITS

State Of Qatar دولة قطر

المجلس الأعلى للصحة
Supreme Council Of Health

Our future lies in our health

www.sch.gov.qa

2003
New Zealand. **Now serving
salads** by DDB Auckland
for McDonald's

2013
United States. By FireHouse
for Farmers Market

2015-A
Qatar. **Our future lies in our
health** by Grey Doha
for Health Ministry

2015-B
Turkey. **Cook slow food fast**
by DDB Istanbul
for Siemens Ovens

2005

inflated-manhood

2008-A

2008-B

2005

China. By JodyXiong
Shanghai *for Pfizer Viagra*

2008-A

New Zealand. *The world's
biggest penis* by DraftFCB
for PrimeTV - True Stories

2008-B

France. By Ogilvy & Mather
Paris *for État Libre d'Orange
Perfume*

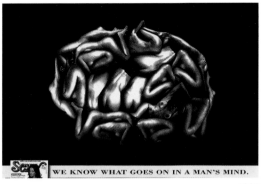

#naked-truth

WE KNOW WHAT GOES ON IN A MAN'S MIND.

1997

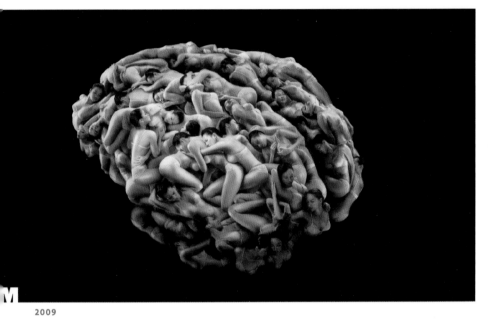

2009

1997
Brazil. *We know what goes on in a man's mind* by Fischer Justus Total *for Sexy Magazine*

2009
Singapore.
By Ogilvy & Mather *for FHM*

heavy-lookalike

FITNESS CLUBS

2009

2006

2006
India. By Ogilvy & Mather Mumbai *for Gold's Gym*

2009
Israel. *Search for "Fitness Club"* by Young & Rubicam Tel Aviv *for Yellow Pages*

slim-calendar

2003

2009

2003
Brazil. By Age Comunicações
São Paulo for *Camp Light
Iced Tea*

2009
China. By Group7
for *Flower SPA*

#kiss-my-ass

2009

2013

2009
India. ***Be your own boss***
by JWT for *Dravya
Business Loans*

2013
Romania. ***Be your own boss***
by Graffiti BBDO Bucharest
for *Capital Magazine*

DEAN'S FINEST OLD SCOTCH WHISKY.
SURPRISINGLY MILD.

2010

#mister-monroe

GIN OLD LADY'S :
UN ORIGINAL NÉ EN GRANDE-BRETAGNE.

OLD LADY'S
LONDON
DRY GIN

L'ABUS D'ALCOOL EST DANGEREUX POUR LA SANTÉ . CONSOMMEZ AVEC MODÉRATION.

1998

1998
France. By Callegari Berville
Paris *for Old Lady's Dry Gin*

2010
Germany. By Scholz &
Friends *for Dean's Finest
Old Scotch Whisky*

When you smoke so do our patients.

ABSOLUTELY NO SMOKING ON CAPITAL HEALTH PROPERTY.

2007-B

Stop second hand smoking

2007-A

SMOKE-FREE HOME

2008-A

smoking-child

2008-B

2008

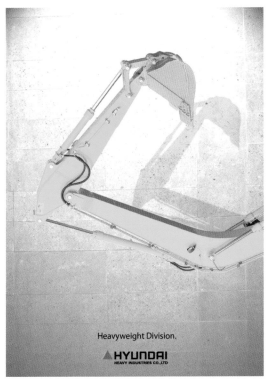

2008
Germany. By DDB Berlin
for Volkswagen Cross Polo

2011
Australia. By DDB Sydney
for Volkswagen Tiguan

2011

2009

2008
Algeria. By JWT Alger
for Hyundai Heavyweight

2009
Bulgaria. By Publicis
Marc *for JCB – Super
natural power*

2012

#express

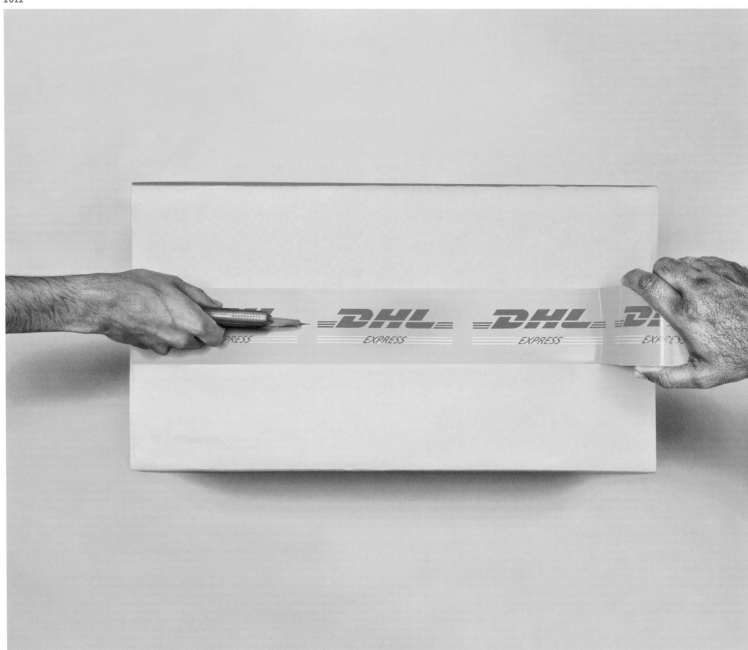

2015

2012
Brazil. By AlmapBBDO
for Gollog Express Delivery

2015
India. By Grey Bangalore
for DHL Express

fishman

STOP CLIMATE CHANGE
BEFORE IT CHANGES YOU.

WWF
for a living planet`

2008

2013

2008
Belgium. By Germaine
Antwerp *for WWF*

2013
United Kingdom. By Nick
Dynan *for The Nest*

uncrashable

2010

2012

2015

2010
UAE. *Mercedes Distronic
cruise control system
- Through a system of
magnets, small cars are
unable to hit themselves* by
Impact BBDO *for Mercedes*

2012
Singapore. By DDB *for
Volkswagen Tiguan
Automatic Distance Control*

2015
Germany. *The uncrashable
toy car* by Jung von Matt
*for Mercedes Brake Assist
System*

Londres au rabais.
L'aller/retour Paris-Londres : 75€.   eurostar

2002

2007

2002
France. **London cheaper**
by Leg *for Eurostar*
(train tickets promotion)

2007
Germany.
By Scholz & Friends
for HLX.com travels

#piece-of-cake

Your product will look more tempting in La Cucina Italiana.

2007

2009

2007
Brazil. By Lew'Lara TBWA
for Dona Benta Flour

2009
Italy. By D'Adda, Lorenzini,
Vigorelli, BBDO Milan *for*
La cucina italiana magazine

2007

2008

glass-breaker

2014

2007
Canada. ***Don't make it a grad to forget*** by Calder Bateman Edmonton *for MADD - Don't drink & drive*

2008
New Zealand. By Saatchi & Saatchi *for Road Safety*

2014
Uganda. ***Don't drink and drive*** by Fireworks *for Road Safety*

2005

2005

2008

weak-arms

2013

2013

2005
United States.
By BBDO New York
for *The Sopranos / HBO*

2008
The Netherlands.
By New Message
Amsterdam *for Tarantino
"Death Proof" DVD*

2013
Canada. **By WAX Calgary**
for Calgary Horror Con

2011

#strong-arms

2013

2015

2011
Switzerland. By Saatchi &
Saatchi Simko *for Voltaren*

2013
Indonesia. By Publicis
Jakarta *for Neo
Rheumacyl Forte*

2015
United States. By Gyro
Chicago *for John Deere*

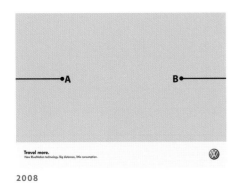

Travel more.
New BlueMotion technology. Big distances, little consumption.

2008

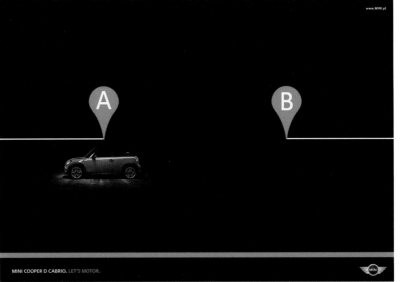

www.MINI.pt

driving-distance

MINI COOPER D CABRIO. LET'S MOTOR.

2011

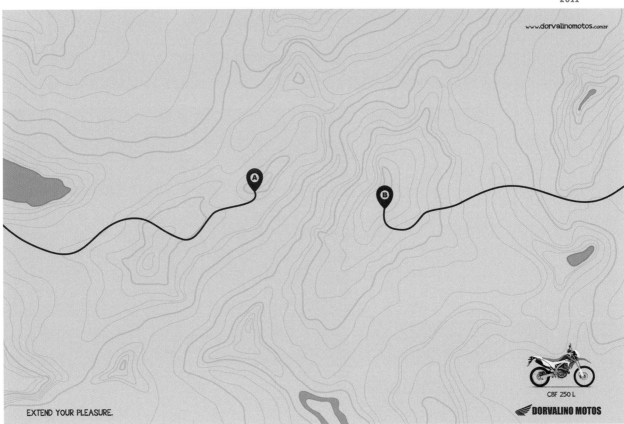

www.dorvalinomotos.com.br

EXTEND YOUR PLEASURE.

CBF 250 L

DORVALINO MOTOS

2013

2008
Italy. *Travel more*
by DDB Milan *for*
Volkswagen BlueMotion

2011
Portugal. *Enjoy the ride*
by Young & Rubicam Lisbon
for BMW Mini Cabrio

2013
Brazil. *Extend your pleasure*
by 9mm Propaganda
for Dorvalino Motos

#smash-up

2007

2014

2007
Thailand. By V2 Power
Bangkok *for Bendix Brakes*

2014
Germany. By Scholz &
Friends Hamburg
*for Opel / Forward
collision alert system*

#bbq-special

2012

2011

2011
Mexico. By DDB Mexico
City *for Volkswagen
Original Parts*

2012
South Africa. By Ogilvy &
Mather *for Volkswagen
Genuine Parts*

2008

[Trash] that makes you want to pick up trash?!

Reflection Project
~ Reflect on our lifestyle ~

2012-A

2012-B

giant-butts

TOBACCO
WEIGHS ANNUALLY
47 BILLION €URO
ON FRENCH SOCIETY

CNCT
NATIONAL COMMITTEE
AGAINST TOBACCO

cnct.fr

2008
Germany. By BBDO
for Anti-Smoking
Organization

2012-A
Japan. By Grey Tokyo
for Reflection Project

2012-B
France. By TBWA Paris
for SNCF

2013
Italy. For Fondazione
Umberto Veronesi

2014
France. By BETC Paris
for Anti-Tobacco INPES

2007

2003

2003
Peru. By BBDO
for Alka-Seltzer

2007
Singapore. By JWT
for Alka-Seltzer

#sleeping-beauty

2007

2011

2007
UAE. ***Stay Young*** by Team
Young & Rubicam Dubai
for A4 (Al Tayer)
Age Reversal Cream

2011
Switzerland. ***Forever Young***
by Publicis Zurich
for Garnier Ultra Lift Cream

#inner-beauty

2008

2013-A

2013-B

2008
Malaysia. By Publicis *for Nike*

2013-A
Estonia. By Tabasco
for Rademar

2013-B
Brazil. By Young & Rubicam
for Sao Paulino

2005

2005

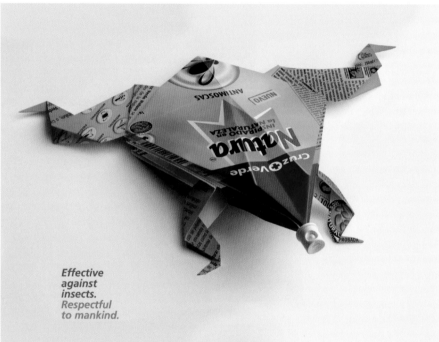

Effective
against
insects.
Respectful
to mankind.

predators

2009

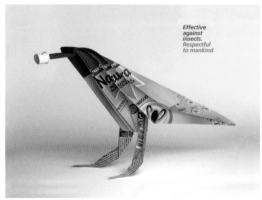

Effective
against
insects.
Respectful
to mankind.

2009

2005

South Africa. By The
Jupiter Drawing Room
Johannesburg
for Target Insecticide

2009

Spain. By Grey Barcelona
for Natura Insecticide

beer-belly

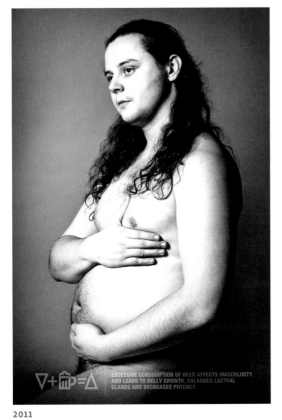

2011

2016

2011

Russia. *Excessive consumption of beer affects masculinity...* by M&C Saatchi Moscow *for Akzia Student Journal anti drinking campaign*

2016

Germany. *Brewed with love* by Jung von Matt Hamburg *for Bergedorfer Beer*

hands-up

2000

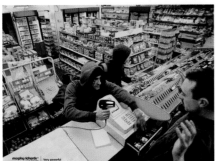

2006

2010

2000

Spain. By Remo Asatsu *for 13th Street TV channel*

2006

India. *Very powerful* by Contract Mumbai for *Morphy Richards Hair Dryers*

2010

France. By Kuryo *for Leroy Merlin*

#headache

2005

Aspirin ads were wrapped on the backs of buses all around the city of Toronto. The ads used brake lights to exaggerate the pain caused by headaches. When the buses braked, the lights lit up to highlight the throbbing pain. As Toronto is one of the worst cities for traffic, the message especially hit home for commuters stuck behind these buses.

⊕ **ASPIRIN.**

2011

2005

Brazil. *For that annoying headache that comes and goes* by JWT São Paulo for Saridon

2011

Canada. *Extra strength for headaches* by BBDO Toronto *for Aspirin*

#catch-of-the-day

2007

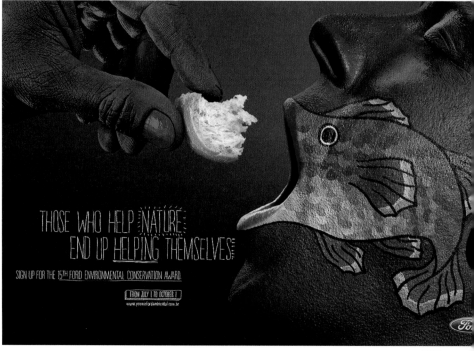

THOSE WHO HELP NATURE END UP HELPING THEMSELVES.

SIGN UP FOR THE 15TH FORD ENVIRONMENTAL CONSERVATION AWARD.

FROM JULY 1 TO OCTOBER 1

Ford

2011

2007

Chile. By BBDO *for Eclipse Chewing Gum*

2011

Brazil. By JWT São Paulo *for Ford Corporate Message*

2008

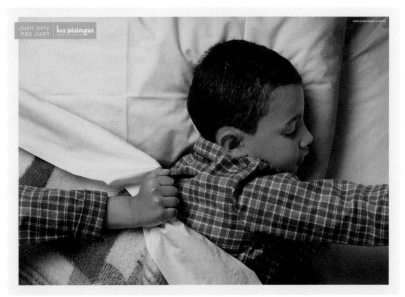

2009

2012

2008
The Netherlands. *You can't expect a child to raise itself* by DDB Amsterdam *for SIRE*

2009
Colombia. *Juan only has Juan* by BBDO Bogota *for Los Pisingos*

2012
Brazil. *Share Mentos if you can* by BBH São Paulo *for Mentos*

2004

#picture-in-picture

2008

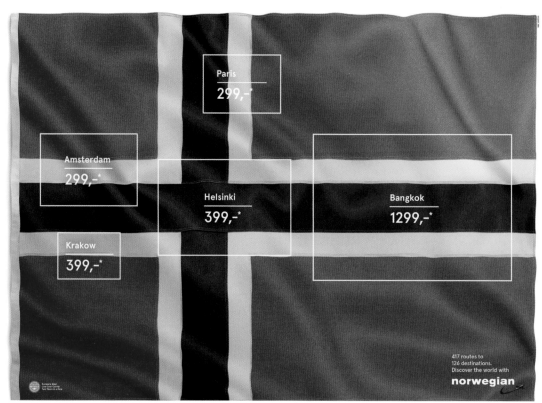

2014

2004
France. *Paris-London: think big* by Leg *for Eurostar*

2008
Poland. *Visit Poland* by Young & Rubicam *for Polish Chamber of Tourism*

2014
Sweden. By M&C Saatchi Stockholm *for Norwegian*

#auto-focus

1983

911

PORSCHE

2013

1983
France. *Oups, I missed the poster* by Publicis Conseil *for Renault 5*

2013
China. By Fred & Farid Shanghai *for Porsche*

key-to-the-city

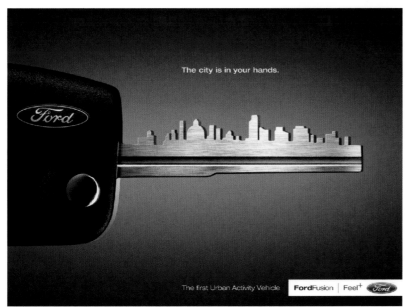

The city is in your hands.

The first Urban Activity Vehicle   FordFusion | Feel⁺ Ford

2008

Turn on your adventure.
Over 620 miles on a single tank. Volkswagen Amarok

2012

2008
Italy. *The city is in your hands* by Ogilvy & Mather *for Ford Fusion*

2012
Peru. *Turn on your adventure* by Below Lima *for Volkswagen Amarok*

#shared-loo

2008

2013

2008

China. **Because you never know who else has been sitting there** by Grey Hong Kong *for Kiwi Kleen toilet cleaner*

2013

Indonesia. **Safe yourself from bad ass** by Grey *for Hygienex (disposable paper toilet seat cover)*

#proven-stability

2007

2010

2007

South Africa. **Shock absorbers** by Joe Public *for Monroe*

2010

Thailand. **For smooth... comfortable ride** by K I D Bangkok *for Dunlop*

AWAKEN
THE CHEMISTRY
GENIUS
THAT LIVES
INSIDE YOU.

suplicy
We love café.

never-sleep

2007

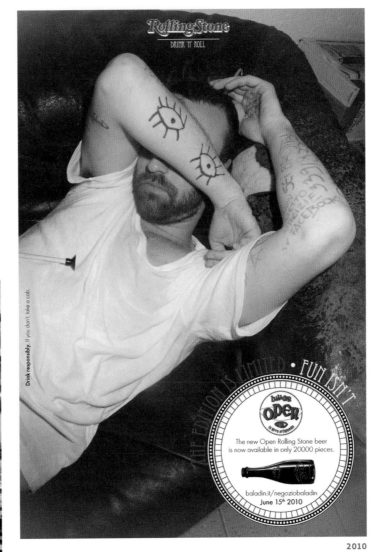

2010

STAY ALERT

PRO PLUS
Caffeine

2011

2014

2007
Brazil. By F/Nazca Saatchi &
Saatchi *for Suplicy Coffee*

2010
Italy. *The edition is limited.*
Fun isn't by BBDO Milan *for*
Open Rolling Stone Beer

2011
United Kingdom. *Stay alert*
by JWT London *for ProPlus*

2014
New Zealand. By DDB
for Steinlager Beer

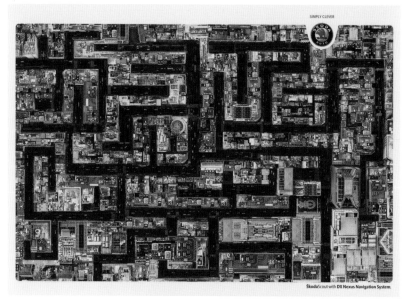

2008-A

escape-the-city

2008-B

2008-C

2008-A
Spain. By Road Publicidade
for Skoda Scout

2008-B
Italy. ***Find your own
way out*** by D'Adda,
Lorenzini, Vigorelli, BBDO
for BMW R 1200

2008-C
Brazil. ***With GPS
as standard***
by Neogama BBH
for Renault Sandero

2006

2007

2008

running-gag

2006
Poland. By Saatchi &
Saatchi Warsaw for
Amnesty International

2007
Brazil. By D/Araújo
Florianópolis for Telephone
Service against domestic
violence

2008
The Philippines. *Anti
Women Abuse* by DM9
DDB for Gabriela

#ironed

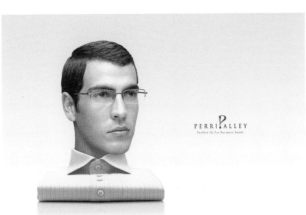

2009

2011

2009
India. By 1pointsize Chennai
for Perri Alley Shirts

2011
UAE. By DDB Dubai
for Vernel Detergent –
Laundry Softener

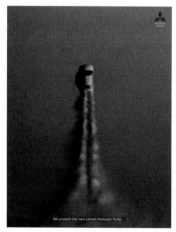

2002

take-off

2012

2013

2002

Chile. *We present the new Lancer Evolution Turbo* by BBDO *for Mitsubishi Lancer*

2012

Turkey. By DDB & Co Istanbul *for KTM Motorbike 450 Rally*

2013

Australia. By Whybin/TBWA Group Melbourne *for Nissan Patrol*

Fruit à-porter

2010

#apple-device

2015

2010
Italy. *Fruit-à-porter* by Euro RSCG Milan *for Vitasnella Fruit Crackers*

2015
France. By Big Family Strasbourg *for Égast*

#in-circles

2004

2006-B

2006-A

2004
South Africa. By NET#WORK BBDO *for Opel Astra Coupé Turbo*

2006-A
Germany. By DDB Berlin *for Volkswagen Golf R32*

2006-B
New Zealand. By Colenso BBDO *for BMW Mini Cooper*

2007

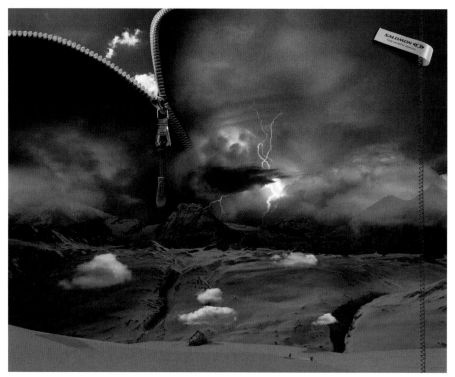

2007

unzip

2010

2014

2014

2007

Spain. By Young & Rubicam
Madrid *for Salomon*
Technical Sportswear

2010

Chile. By Prolam
Young & Rubicam *for*
Columbia Sportswear

2014

Peru. By Saatchi & Saatchi
for Tatoo waterproof jackets

2004

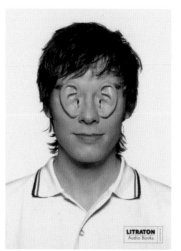

2005

2007

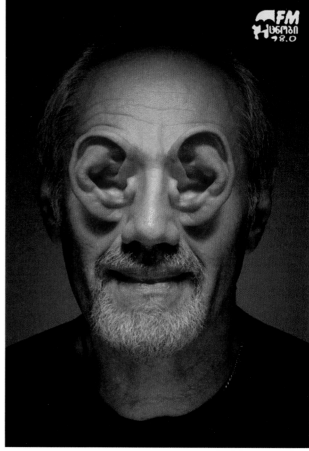

2009

2004
Austria. By Ogilvy & Mather Vienna *for SteinHof Music Production Company*

2005
Germany. *Audio Books* by Springer & Jacoby Hamburg *for Litraton*

2007
United States. By TBWA/ Chiat/Day *for Pioneer*

2009
Georgia. By Sakideamsheni Tbilisi *for 98.0 FM Radio Station*

wake-up-kiss

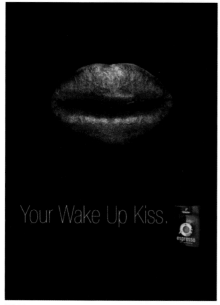

Your Wake Up Kiss.

2004

Botega. Il caffè dal gusto morbido.

2007

2004
Germany. By Scholz &
Friends *for Tchibo
Espresso Coffee*

2007
Italy. By JWT Milan
for Botega Coffee

LLEGARON
LAS
BARATAS
fabricas de francia

2005

#self-defence

THE
HARVEY NICHOLS
SALE
STARTS 27 DECEMBER

2008

2005
Mexico. By DDB Mexico
City *for Fabricas de Francia*

2008
United Kingdom.
By DDB London *for
The Harvey Nichols Sale*

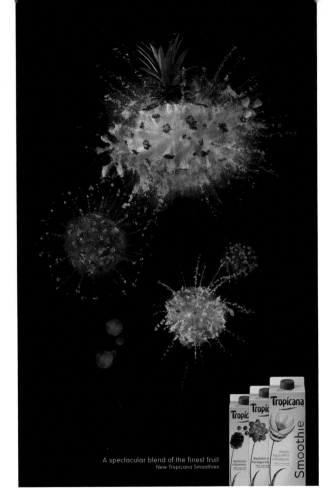

2008

2013

2008
United Kingdom.
A spectacular blend of the finest fruit by DDB London
for Tropicana Smoothies

2013
Thailand. By BBDO Bangkok
for Tefal Blender

2013

distant-forecast

2011

2011
New Zealand. *Today's high in Fiji / 27°C* by Barnes Catmur Auckland
for Fiji Tourism

2013
United States. By Arnold Worldwide *for Carnival Cruise Lines (This billboard ran during NYC winter)*

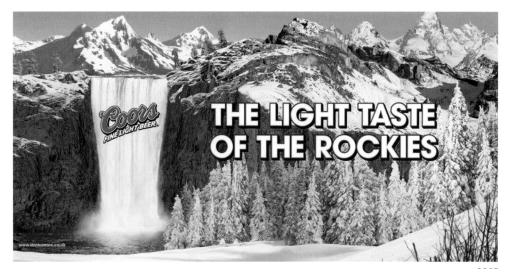

2007

beer-landscapes

2009

2013

2016

2007

United States. **The light taste of the Rockies** for Coors Beer

2009

Poland. By Change *for Tatra Beer (Heineken Group)*

2013

Kazakhstan. **It's ours!** by Ogilvy & Mather for Derbez Beer (Carlsberg)

2016

Peru. *For Cusqueña Beer*

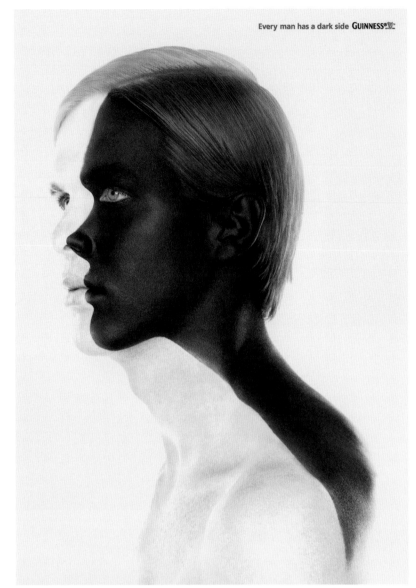

Every man has a dark side GUINNESS®

2009

half-and-half

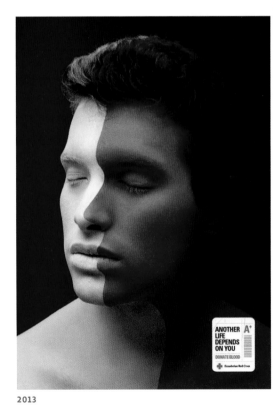

ANOTHER
LIFE
DEPENDS
ON YOU

DONATE BLOOD

A+

Ecuadorian Red Cross

2013

2009
China. By BBDO Shanghai
for Guinness Beer

2013
Ecuador. By McCann Quito
for Ecuadorian Red Cross

1964

human-tripods

2004

IMAGE STABILIZER | **Canon**
LA ESTABILIDAD QUE UNA BUENA FOTO NECESITA

2008

Jeep
THERE'S ONLY ONE

2009

1964
United States.
Human Tripod
by Philippe Halsman

2004
United Kingdom.
By Saatchi & Saatchi London
for Manfrotto Tripods for
Cameras

2008
Chile. By Armstrong &
Asociados Santiago *for
Canon with Image Stabilizer*

2009
Germany. By KNSK *for Jeep*

2003

2013

2003

Brazil. *You'll think your dog's a genius* by Bates for *Perdizes Kennel Dog Training*

2013

United States. *Where every dog's a genius* by Proximity Minneapolis for *Canine College Dog Training*

#breaking-the-wall

2011-A

2011-B

2011-A

United States. *Wear a seat belt* by Esparza Advertising for *New Mexico Road Safety*

2011-B

Russia. *This could be your body* for *Road Safety of Nizhny Novgorod City*

2003

2007

homegrown

2013

2003
Switzerland. ***Very fresh
vegetarian food***
by Wirz Werbung *for Tibits*

2007
France. By Publicis Conseil
for Tefal Vitacuisine

2013
Brazil. By Studio SC São Paulo
*for Festival International de
la Photographie Culinaire*

2008

SUMMERVILLE
SUMMER THE WHOLE YEAR.

2011

2009

2008
Australia. By M&C
Saatchi Sydney *for Tourism
Australia/Direct Marketing*

2009
Colombia. By Young &
Rubicam Bogota
for Falabella Travels

2011
Brazil. *Summer the whole
year* by Gruponove Recife
for SummerVille Resort

comfy

2009-B

2009-A

2009-A
Thailand. *Wake up*
by Oishi Tea *for Oishi Tea*

2009-B
Mexico. *With extra caffeine*
by BBDO *for Pepsi Kick*

#fish-cake

What you eat shouldn't smell like what you ate.

2009

LET IT TASTE THE WAY IT SHOULD

GLAD ClingWrap

KEEP IT FRESH

2011

2009

India. *What you eat shouldn't smell like what you ate* by Euro RSCG Gurgaon *for Finish*

2011

UAE. *Let it taste the way it should* by DDB Dubai *for Glad Cling Wrap*

#yes-they-can

TASTE THE UEFA CHAMPIONS LEAGUE

WIN TICKETS EVERY DAY WITH PEPSI MAX

2016

2014

2014

Chile. ***Official beer of Mexican soccer league*** by Bromley San Antonio *for Coors Light Beer*

2016

United Kingdom. ***Taste the UEFA Champions League*** by AMV BBDO *for Pepsi-Max*

#strike

2010

2006

2006

Germany. By Jung von Matt Hamburg *for Karstadt Quelle Dental Insurance*

2010

Japan. By Dentsu Tokyo *for Ryo Dental Clinic*

Poison the sea, Poison me

2000

Enfrente as ruas.

Novo Gel Kayano **14** Muito mais estabilidade. Melhor do que nunca.

asics
sound mind, sound body

2008

#manhole

Storm Drains are the MOUTH of the River

The river is home to frogs, fish, beavers, birds, and because of carelessness, a diaper wrapped in a plastic grocery bag. Yikes! Remember, **only rain in the storm drain.** timeforcleanwater.com

2013

2000
New Zealand. By Saatchi & Saatchi *for Anti-Pollution, Auckland City Council*

2008
Brazil. ***Face the streets*** by Dez Brasil *for Asics*

2013
United States. By OCCE Reno *for Anti-Pollution, City of Reno*

italian-food

2013

2009

2009

Australia. By Whybin/TBWA
for Sydney Food Festival

2013

Mexico. By Grey Dot *for
Sanborns International
Gourmet Festival*

#mirror-mighty-mirror

2009

2003

2003

Spain. *Narcissist? Maybe...*
by Publicis Casadevall
Barcelona *for Roca Taps*

2009

South Africa. *Beautiful taps*
by FoxP2 Cape Town *for
Isca Taps*

mismatched

2003

2002

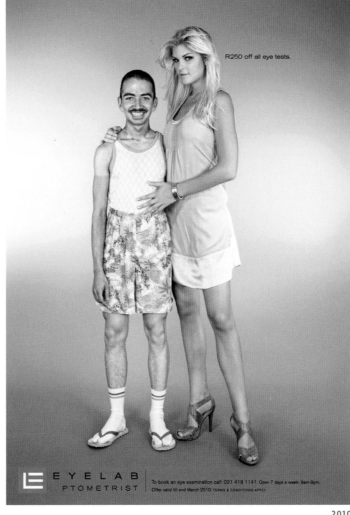

2010

Bulemia and anorexia: the illnesses which are the most like suicide.
anorexie.com

2002

ASSOCIATION QUÉBÉCOISE D'AIDE AUX PERSONNES
SOUFFRANT D'ANOREXIE NERVEUSE ET DE BOULIMIE
1 801 630 0907

2004

Foto: Bruno Ribeiro

2008

2010

Bulimia mata.

Clínica Delfin
DIAGNÓSTICO POR IMAGEM

A bulimia nervosa e a anorexia
causam inúmeras mortes no
Brasil. O diálogo transparente é o
melhor remédio para tratar deste
assunto. Converse com seus
familiares e procure um médico.

Resp. Téc.: Dr. Delfin Gonzales Miranda - CRM 4875

2002
France. By FCB
for Anorexie.com

2004
Canada. By Amen for Aneb

2008
Brazil. By Única
for Clínica Delfin

2010
Czech Republic. By Ogilvy &
Mather Prague for Anabell

2011-A

#burned-calories

2011-B

2011-A
Canada. By BleuBlancRouge
for Gold's Gym Sports Club

2011-B
Brazil. By JWT Curitiba
for Gustavo Borges
Swimming & Fitness
Academy

#sliding-pigs

2003

2010

2003

Brazil. *No food sticks to it* by
Saatchi & Saatchi São Paulo
for Tefal/T-Fal frying pan

2010

India. By McCann Erickson
Mumbai *for Nirlep
Non-Stick Pans*

#hands-down

2011

2014

2011

Switzerland. By Ruf Lanz
for Suva accident prevention

2014

Vietnam. By Datviet
Riverorchid *for Green Cross
Hand Sanitizer*

Turn this into an endangered species. **Keep the beaches clean.**

2003

HELP US KEEP THE OCEAN CLEAN
www.surfrider.fr

2005

deeply-similar

This year the ocean's biggest killer will be the rubbish you leave behind. Help us protect our precious coastlines, marine animals and seabirds and join a SAS beach clean near you.

sas.org.uk

SURFERS AGAINST SEWAGE

2014

Homo Ignorantis
Help them go extinct.

JEAN-MICHEL COUSTEAU'S
OCEAN FUTURES BRASIL

2015

2003
Puerto Rico. **Turn this into an endangered species. Keep the beaches clean** by McCann Erickson Guaynabo *for Scuba Dogs Association*

2005
France. **Help us keep the ocean clean** by Young & Rubicam Paris *for Surfrider Foundation*

2014
United Kingdom. By HJ London *for Surfers Against Sewage*

2015
Brazil. By Young & Rubicam *for Jean-Michel Cousteau's Ocean Futures*

2007

2007

Singapore. By Publicis
for Bic Extra Fine

2009

2009

Venezuela. By Young &
Rubicam Caracas
for Papermate Extra Fine

#pull-over

2013

2014

2013

France. *To survive, patients
must rely on family
solidarity* by TBWA Paris
*for Rose Mag / Cancer
awareness*

2014

Colombia. *Some clothes
can heal, donate one item,
help kids with cancer* by
Sancho BBDO Bogota *for El
Ropero*

2003

the everyday exotic.

enjoy your exotic moment responsibly.

KAHLÚA

2006

best-friend

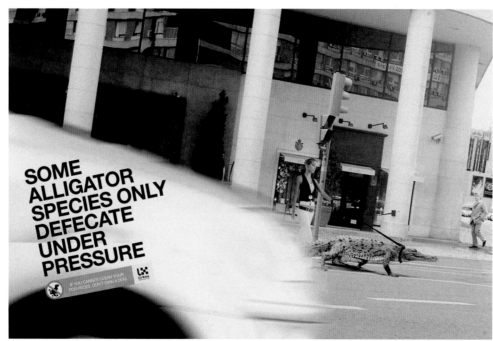

SOME
ALLIGATOR
SPECIES ONLY
DEFECATE
UNDER
PRESSURE

2009

2003

Belgium. By Young &
Rubicam *for Land Rover*

2006

United States. By Publicis
for Kahlúa

2009

Portugal. By Andre Lopes
for Lisbon City Council

ghettoblaster

2008-A

2008-B

2008-A
Brazil. By Young & Rubicam
São Paulo *for LG Car Audio*

2008-B
South Africa. By FCB
*for Toyota Yaris with
Rockford Fosgate Sound*

#closer-look

2001

2013

2001
Brazil. By Age Brazil
for Bravo Magazine

2013
United States. **Get a world
view** by BBDO New York *for
The Economist*

HILTL
VEGETARIAN RESTAURANT

#slurp

2002

2012

2002

Belgium. By Duval
Guillaume Brussels *for*
Double Swiss Fresh / Quick
Restaurants

2012

Switzerland. By Ruf Lanz *for*
Hiltl Vegetarian Restaurant

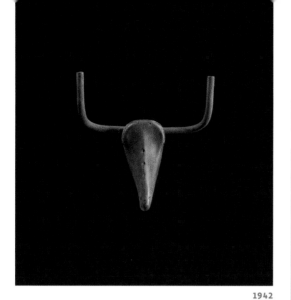

1942

2014-A

2000

2014-B

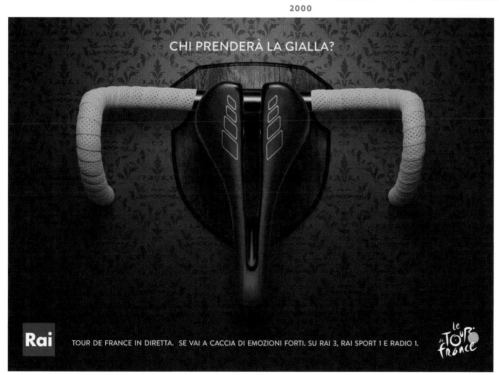

CHI PRENDERÀ LA GIALLA?

Rai   TOUR DE FRANCE IN DIRETTA. SE VAI A CACCIA DI EMOZIONI FORTI. SU RAI 3, RAI SPORT 1 E RADIO 1.

le TOUR de France

2016

1942
Bull's head
by Pablo Picasso

2000
Spain. *Spain cycling tour*
by FCB Tapsa Madrid
for TVE

2014-A
Brazil. *Hunted on the road*
by Heads Propaganda Rio
for Road Safety

2014-B
Austria. *Upcycle fetish/*
Tribute to Picasso
by Andreas Scheiger

2016
Italy. By Young & Rubicam
for Rai

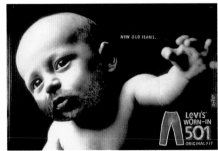

2000

old-youngsters

2010

2011

cooking-symphony

2001

2006

2001
Spain. By Euro RSCG
for Castafiore Restaurant

2006
Canada. ***From cooking
to classical*** by MacLaren
McCann Calgary *for Epcor*

#super-potato

2008

2009

2008
Brazil. By Fields
for Sabugosa Bookstore

2009
United States. By LatinWorks
Austin *for Active Life
Movement*

shorter

2011

2014

2011
Luxembourg.
By Concept Factory *for*
Tango Vodafone Roaming

2014
Kazakhstan. ***Don't shorten***
your travel story by Red
for Beeline Roaming Service

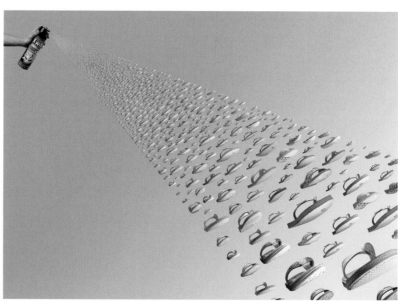

2009

sprayed

2005

2005
Uruguay. By DDB
for Selton Insecticide

2009
UAE. By Fortune
Promoseven Dubai
for Kwik Insecticide

2004

chicken-origamis

2007

2012

2004
United States. By Joseph
Wu for McDonald's
Chicken McGrill

2007
United Kingdom. By TBWA
London for Whiskas Chicken

2012
Finland. By DDB Helsinki
for McDonald's
Chicken Burger

#long-neck

2006

2009

2006
United States. By BBDO West *for San Francisco Zoo*

2009
United Kingdom. By Robson Brown Ltd. Newcastle *for Chester Zoo*

drilling

2004

2007

2004
United States. Student work by Metin Sozen, New York (awarded Bronze at the Andy Awards) *for Milwaukee Tools*

2007
India. *Drills through anything* by Vyas Giannetti Creative *for Blue Point Power Tools*

2013-A

time-machine

2013-A

2013-B

2013-A
France. By BETC Paris
for Evian

2013-B
Canada. By Cloud Raker
Montreal *for Natrel Milk*

2007

open-close

Sees in case you don't.
The predictive safety system Audi pre sense.

2011

2014

YOU CAN'T FAKE BEING AWAKE.

2015

2013

2007
China. By JWT Shanghai *for Lipton Tea*

2011
Germany. ***Sees in case you don't*** by Kempertrautmann Hamburg *for Audi*

2013
Brazil. By Z Plus *for Groove Energy Drink*

2014
France. ***Always keep an eye on the road*** by Young & Rubicam Paris *for Opel*

2015
Germany. By Miami Ad School Berlin *for Red Bull*

2007

Threatened animals
are not the only ones
in need of donations.

Thank you for your help. The home for the blind in Zurich. PO account 80-21096-3. **www.muehlehalde.ch**   mühlehalde

2009

2010

2007
France. *Turn your family
into a protected species*
by M&C Saatchi *for La Poste*

2009
Switzerland. *A place to help
blind people* by Ruf Lanz
for Mühlehalde

2010
Argentina. *People with
disabilities are not so hot in
the news as panda bears,
but they also need your
help* by McCann Erickson
*for Fundación Par – to help
people with disabilities*

September 11 every day

Why don't we call it terrorism?
www.draugiem.lv/neputmiglu

2013

2008

2008
New Zealand. **Terrorism related deaths since 2001: 11,337. Tobacco related deaths since 2001: 30,000,000** by DDB for ASH Anti-Tobacco

2013
Lettonia.
By Neputmiglu Anti-Tobacco for Neputmiglu

2012

2003

2003
Brazil. By F/Nazca Saatchi & Saatchi for Arno (SEB Group) Vacuum Cleaner

2012
South Africa. By Canvas for A&A Furnishers/Bosch

2008-A

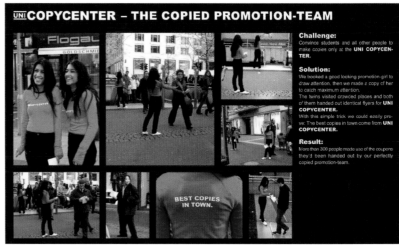

2008-B

identical-twins

2009

2008-A

The Netherlands. **Perfect copies** by Young & Rubicam *for Xerox*

2008-B

Germany. **Twin promotion team** by DDB Düsseldorf *for UNI-Copycenter*

2009

Portugal. **Perfect copies twins with flyers** by Leo Burnett Lisbon *for Staples*

#frogman

2009

2002

2002

Germany. **Make yourself unattractive** by Scholz & Friends Berlin *for Pellit Insect-repellent*

2009

Singapore. **Change the way insects see you** by McCann Erickson *for Repella Insect Repeller*

2007

2007

silver-generation

2008

2008

2007

Brazil. *By DPZ for Sadia Light Meals*

2008

Spain. ***You'll forget about meat*** *by Grey Barcelona for Florette. Sealed gourmet salads.*

Illegal logging kills more than just trees.

2008

2005

2005
Germany. By Ogilvy &
Mather Frankfurt *for WWF*

2008
United Kingdom. *Illegal
logging kills more than
just trees* by Kitcatt Nohr
London *for WWF*

2013-A

self-centred-dogs

2013-B

2014

2013-A
Brazil. By Tuppi
for Pet Beauty

2013-B
Chile. **For better looking
dogs** by Porta Santiago for
Champion Pet Food

2014
Turkey. By Ogilvy & Mather
for Ford Rearview Camera

brain-teaser

**We're looking for computer engineers who like to solve difficult problems.
Call us on this number now:**

2004

**We're looking for engineers who like to solve difficult problems.
Call us on this number now:**
x = 24, y = 30
Phone = 044.(y²−x).(y²−10²)×10.

2008

If you have what it takes to be an engineer in the Air Force call the number below.

AIR FORCE ACCOMPLISHED

2014

2004
Switzerland. By Ruf Lanz Zurich *for McKinsey & Company Engineers Recruitment*

2008
Switzerland. By Ruf Lanz *for Engineers Recruitment*

2014
Australia. By Young & Rubicam *for Air Force Recruitment*

nose-to-nose

2005

Força instantânea.

2009

2005
India. ***Now in Egypt*** by Ogilvy & Mather *for Fevicol Glue*

2009
Portugal. By DDB Lisbon *for Henkel Loctite Super Glue Power Gel*

sex-addict

he right placement can make quite a difference.

M E D I A 1
Media planning

2008

2008
France. By Ogilvy & Mather
Paris *for Perrier Mix*

2009
Austria. ***The right
placement can make quite
a difference*** by Demner,
Merlicek & Bergmann
Vienna *for Media 1*

creative-heights

2001

2001
Argentina. By DDB
for Mitsubishi Rally

2003

2003
France. By Young & Rubicam
Paris *for Land Rover*

2007

2007
Bolivia. By BBDO
for Volkswagen

new-hand

2004

2008

2004
France. By Publicis Conseil
for Calor Maneis

2008
Australia. By JWT Sydney
for Purell

2015-A

2015-C

2015-B

SIEMENS

ODORS OUT

2015-D

2015-A

Germany. *The Architect* by Erik Johansson

2015-B

Chile. *Let the smell out and the taste in* by Museo for Haier

2015-C

Indonesia. By Dentsu *for Panasonic Ventilation Solutions*

2015-D

Turkey. *Odors out* by Medina Turgul DDB *for Siemens Extractor*

#pedestrian

Não envie SMS ao dirigir.

2012

2014

2012
Brazil. *You can hit more than a key when you text and drive* by Heitor Buchalla Portfolio Work / Unreleased *for Volkswagen*

2014
Brazil. *Don't text & drive* by Ideia3 Salvador *for Ford*

dirty-sushi

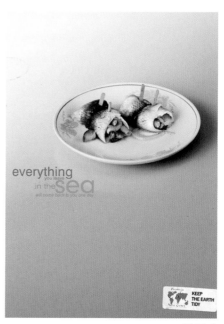

everything
you leave
in the sea
will come back to you, one day

2001

2008-A

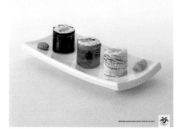

2008-B

2001
Japan. *Help us keep the ocean clean* by Hakuhodo *for WWF*

2008-A
Poland. *Keep the earth tidy* by JWT Warsaw *for Fundacja Nasza Ziemia*

2008-B
UAE. By JWT Dubai *for Emirates Environmental Group*

2006

nessie

2009

2012

2006

Israel. *Is it real?* by Young & Rubicam *for Mercedes CL-Class*

2009

UAE. *Experience the unusual* by DDB Gulf *for Volkswagen Scirocco*

2012

Brazil. By Prósper Comunicação Vitória *for Vitoriawagen Imports*

saigon yoga - "stretching time"

2006

time-to-stretch

2007

2006
Vietnam. *Stretching time*
by JWT *for Saigon Yoga*

2007
China. By Lem Shanghai
for Y+ Yoga Center

mini-me

2005

2007

2003

2003
Argentina. By DDB Buenos
Aires *for Philips D-Wide*

2005
Germany. By Springer &
Jacoby *for Men & kid's shoes
by GÖRTZ Stores*

2007
Belgium. By DDB Brussels
*for Men & kid's wear at
C&A stores*

2004

BUGS
PEST CONTROL

2006

#and-jerry

You
definitely
notice
its lack.

www.olivepier.com

2011

2004

Germany. *Pest exterminators* by Grey for *Schädlingsbekämpfung*

2006

Bolivia. *Pest control* by Freelo Santa Cruz *for Bugs*

2011

Turkey. By Works *for Olive Pier Oil*

2007-A

homeless

2007-B

2009

2010

2012

reasonpartners.org

2012

2007-A

Finland. **You can help stop global warming** by Euro RSCG Helsinki *for WWF*

2007-B

Chile. **Global warming is leaving many homeless** by Draft FCB + IDB Santiago *for Fundacion Ecoeduca*

2009

Canada. By Reason Partners *for Reason Partners*

2010

United Kingdom. By WCRS *for Born Free*

2012

United Kingdom. Written and directed by Michael Goeghegan *for Greenpeace (TV Commercial)* Video Link: youtu.be/4xpfø4nximl

COPY PASTE — **135**

2003

2008

lightness

2013

2003

Kazakhstan. By Bright
Colors Advertising
for Coca-Cola Light

2008

Belgium. By Air Brussels
for Schweppes Agrum Light

2013

Turkey. ***Very light oil***
by KAF Ankara
for Sunar Corn Oil

#handcuffed

2009

2008

2008

Australia. *Graffiti and your next stop could be jail* by Cooch Creative Perth *for Western Australia's transport authority*

2009

Switzerland. *Victims are people just like you and me* by Advico Young & Rubicam *for Acat.ch*

competitor-bashing

2007

2009

2007

Germany. By Jung von Matt *for DHL*

2009

United States. By Marked for Trade Charlotte *for DASH Courier service*

mouth-to-mouth

2012

2014

2012
Russia. By Voskhod
Yekaterinburg *for
Make the politicians work*

2014
United States. By Saatchi &
Saatchi New York
for Crossroads Charity

#show-off

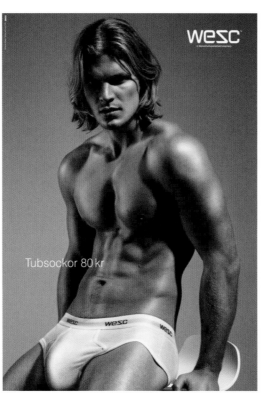

2006

2008

2006
Sweden. By King
Stockholm *for WESC
street & underwear*

2008
Belgium. By DDB Brussels
for Deleye Fashion Store

2005

2006

uncovered-truth

2010

2011

2012

2005
The Philippines. By JWT
for Ford Focus

2006
Peru. By Positivo Pragma
DDB Lima *for Toyota Yaris*

2010
Brazil. By Samba Pro /
Neogama BBH
for Renault Clio

2011
Canada. By Taxi2 Toronto
for BMW Mini

2012
France. By Prodeo
for Kia Cee'd

COPY PASTE — **139**

2011

TRUE SOUND **BANG & OLUFSEN**

2010

2010

France. ***True sound*** by
Ogilvy & Mather Paris *for
Bang & Olufsen*

2011

Switzerland. ***Purest sound
quality*** by Ruf Lanz
for Selmi Tonstudio Zurich

#gimme-a-hand

WHOSE HAND ARE YOU HOLDING?

2008

2010

2008

Australia. By Euro RSCG *for
Dettol Hand Gel*

2010

Thailand. ***What you really
touch?*** by Chuo Senko *for
Sanzer Hand Gel*

seagull

2008

2013

2008
Australia. *After 70
years we've seen it all*
by Clemenger BBDO
Melbourne *for Mutual
Community Health
Insurance*

2013
France. By Change
for Takoon Kiteboarding

AND WHAT DOES YOUR GARBAGE SAY ABOUT YOU?
Sort your waste. Think, what a mess you're leaving behind for others to live in.

Ministry of Environment

2009

#hidden-message

Littering says a lot about yo

TORONTO Livegre

2014

2009
Poland. *And what does your garbage say about you?* by Young & Rubicam Warsaw *for Polish Ministry of Environment*

2014
Canada. *Littering says a lot about you* by Publicis *for Livegreen Toronto*

2011

2011

2013

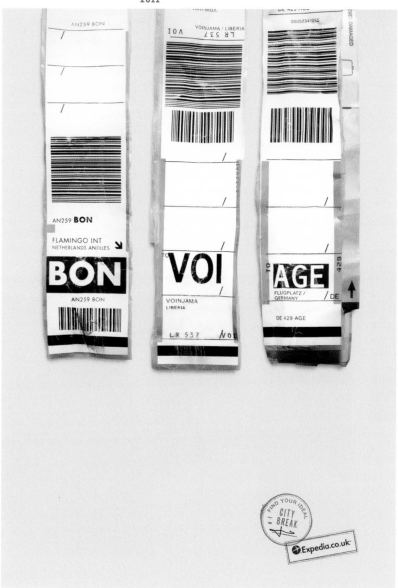

2013

2011
Germany. By BBDO
Düsseldorf *for Bayer Aspirin*

2013
United Kingdom.
By Ogilvy & Mather
for Expedia Travels

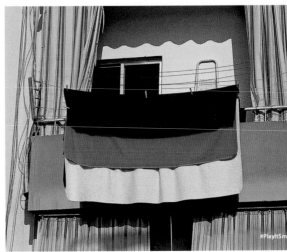

2014

2006

2006
Germany. *For a country that rediscovered its colours this summer* (during FIFA worldcup) by BBDO Düsseldorf *for Persil*

2014
Lebanon. By Leo Burnett Beyrouth *for Bonux*

smack

2001

2007

2001
Spain. *No smint, no kiss* by Tandem DDB *for Smint*

2007
Sweden. By McCann Erickson Stockholm *for The Coca-Cola Company*

2008

#destinations

2010

2008
Portugal. *Lisbon airport has a new look* by BBDO Lisbon for Ana Aeroportos Lisboa

2010
Germany. By BBDO for Braun Satin Hair Brush

#sea-pool

2010

2009

2009
Canada. By LG2 *for New Brunswick tourism office*

2010
Mexico. By Gaudelli MCW *for Riu Hotels and Resorts*

2007

#jurassic-loads

2009

2007
Mexico. By Z Publicidade *for Volkswagen Crafter*

2009
Chile. By La Mesa Santiago *for Volkswagen Transporter*

2003

2003

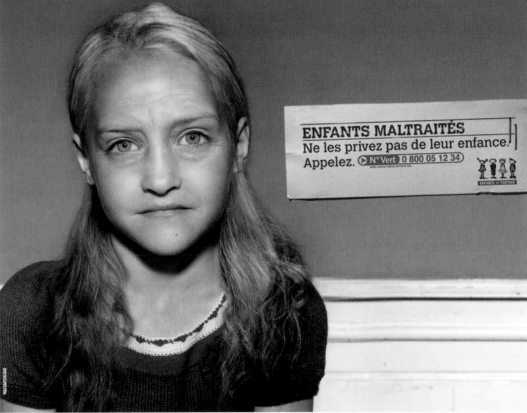

2009

#fast-ageing

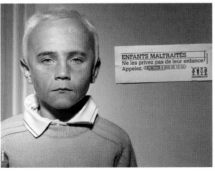

2009

2003
United Kingdom. *Abuse through prostitution steals children lives* by BBH *for Barnardo's*

2009
France. *Abused childs. Don't deprive them of their childhood* by M&C Saatchi GAD *for Enfance et partage*

shrinking

2006-B

2006-A

2006-A
Venezuela. By Leo Burnett
for Lido, Gym Spa

2006-B
Japan. By JWT
for Kellogg's Special K

#kiss-kiss

2005

2011

2005
The Netherlands. **Classic rock** by Leo Burnett
Amsterdam *for City FM 87.6*

2011
Brazil. ***Ten years honouring the rock classics*** by Lua
Branca São Paulo *for Kiss FM*

2008

2008

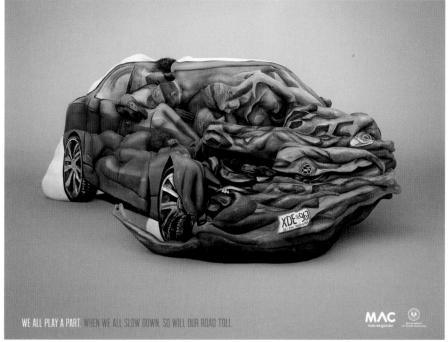

WE ALL PLAY A PART. WHEN WE ALL SLOW DOWN, SO WILL OUR ROAD TOLL.

MAC

2012

#rein-car-nation

2013

2006-A

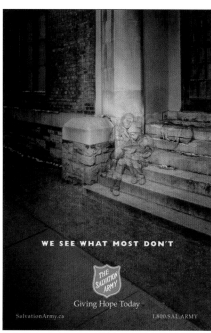

2006-B

2006-B

2007

#not-seen-not-caught

2012

2012

ALWAYS THIRSTY. Bounty

2011

One sheet is enough. Foxy ULTRA

2016

2011
United States. *Always thirsty* by Publicis New York for *Bounty absorbent paper*

2016
Italy. *One sheet is enough* by Lowe Pirelli Milan for *Foxy Ultra absorbent paper*

half-preserved

2014

2008

2008
India. By Sudler & Hennessey Mumbai for *Wildlife SOS*

2014
Uganda. By Scanad Kampala for *Airtel*

2007-A

2007-B

candy-crash

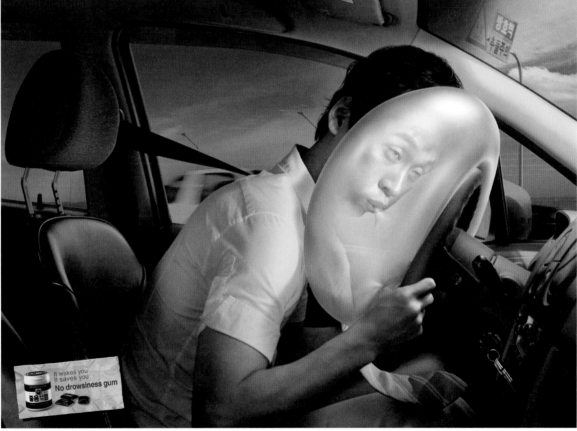

2008

2002

absorbent

2010

2014

2002

Brazil. By DPZ São Paulo
for Chifon Paper Towels

2010

Germany. By Counterpart
GmbH *for Rewe*

2014

India. By McCann Erickson
*for Premier Absorbent
Paper Towels*

154 — COPY PASTE

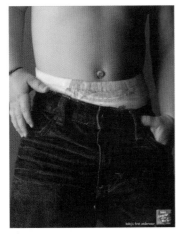

2004

2008

baggy-pants

2005

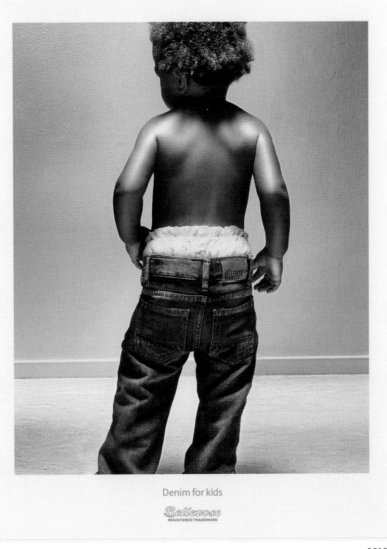

Denim for kids

Bellerose
REGISTERED TRADEMARK

2010

2004
France. By Saatchi & Saatchi
for Pampers

2005
Argentina. By Craverolanis
for Babysec Nappies

2008
Germany. By Saatchi &
Saatchi Frankfurt
for Pampers Nappies

2010
Belgium. By Happiness
Brussels *for Bellerose
Denims for kids*

#shortcut

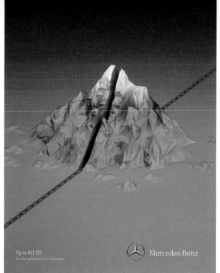

2013

2009

2009

Malaysia. By Young &
Rubicam Kuala Lumpur
for Volkswagen Touareg

2013

Austria. By Jung von Matt
for Mercedes-Benz G-Class

fast-life

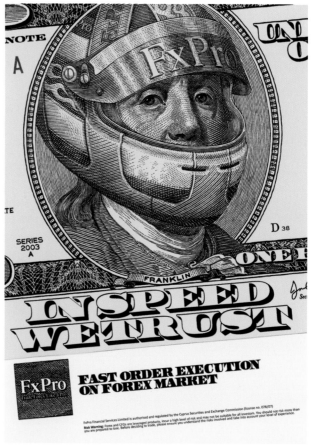

2010

2003

2003

Austria. By Jung von Matt
Vienna *for Bank Austria
Creditanstalt Financial
Advisers*

2010

Russia. ***Fast order execution
on forex market*** by Freeger
Moscow *for FX Pro*

Calvé béarnaise sauce. Delicious on fish.

1999

yummy-myself-and-i

2007-A

Vis, zoveel lekkers dat er is.

2007-B

1999
The Netherlands. **Delicious on fish** by Lintas *for Calvé Béarnaise Sauce*

2007-A
Canada. By WAX Calgary *for Historic Lynchburg Sauce*

2007-B
Belgium. By Mortier Brigade *for Vlam*

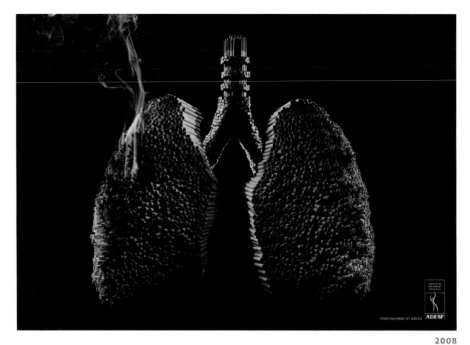

2008

#smoked

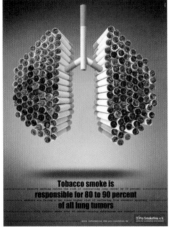

2005

Tobacco smoke is responsible for 80 to 90 percent of all lung tumors

2005
Germany. **Anti-smoking** by Fahrnholz & Junghanns & Raetzel Munich
for Pro smokefree

2008
Brazil. By Neogama BBH *for ADESF association to help smokers*

#melting

2006

2010

2006

2006
Germany. **Homeless ice sculpture** by Aimaq Rapp Stolle Berlin *for Berlin City Mission*

2010
France. **Homeless ice sculpture** by BDDP Unlimited Paris *for Fondation Abbé Pierre*

women-penis

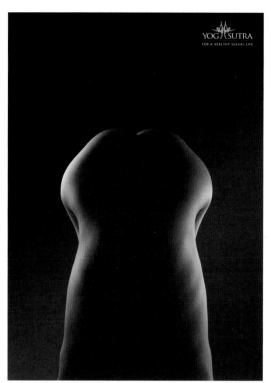

2012

USE CONDOM BEFORE SCREWING UP!

Unprotected sex is responsible for 80-85% of HIV transmisson.
7 Hills Foundation supports the fight against AIDS.

7 HILLS
foundation
www.7hillsfoundation.nl

2011

2011
Turkey. By THE Agency
Istanbul *for 7 Hills
Foundation /
Aids Prevention*

2012
India. *For a healthy
sexual life* by Publicis
Communications Mumbai
for Yog Sutra

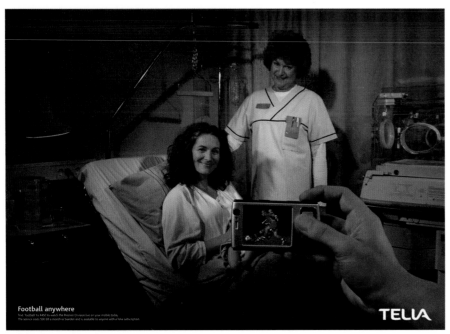

Football anywhere
Text: Football to 44511 to watch the Premier Division live on your mobile today.
The service costs SEK 69 a month in Sweden and is available to anyone with a Telia subscription.

TELIA

#unworthy-father

2007

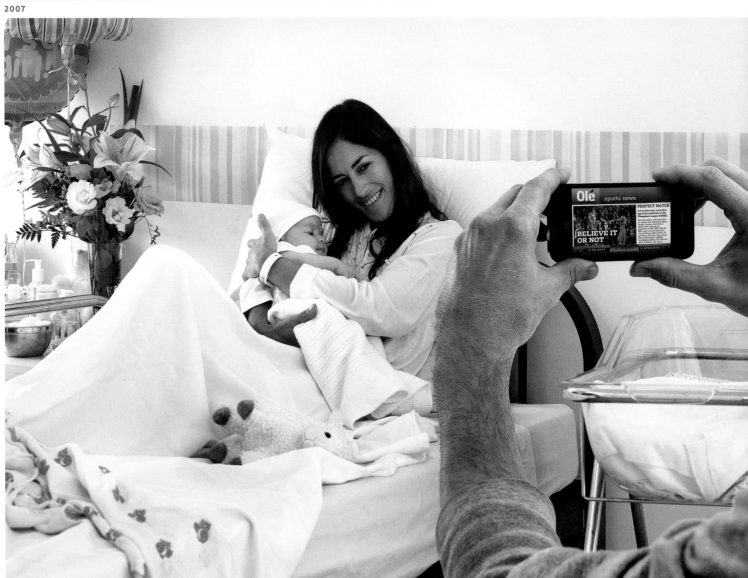

Olé sports news
PERFECT MATCH
BELIEVE IT OR NOT

2013

2007
Sweden. *Football
everywhere* by McCann
Erickson Stockholm *for Telia*

2013
Argentina. By Young &
Rubicam Buenos Aires *for
Olé Sports News*

1996

#hello-submarine

2013-A

2013-B

1996
Sweden. By Young &
Rubicam *for Gevalia
(KraftFoods)*

2013-A
Italy. By M&C Saatchi Milan
for Europe Assistance Milan

2013-B
United States. By Lead Dog
Los Angeles for
"The Americans" Spy Series

#second-hand-feet

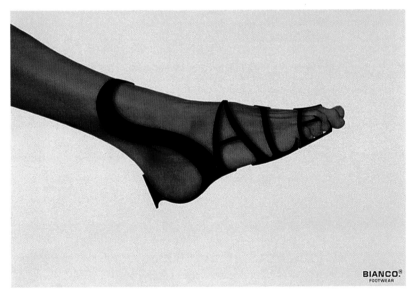

2001

2010

2001
Denmark. *Sale*
by & Co Copenhagen
for Bianco Footwear

2010
Kuwait. *Up to 50% sale*
by Talent *for Essere*

elongated-glasses

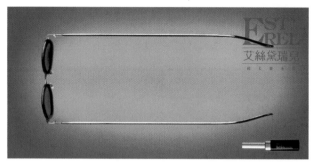

2001

2007

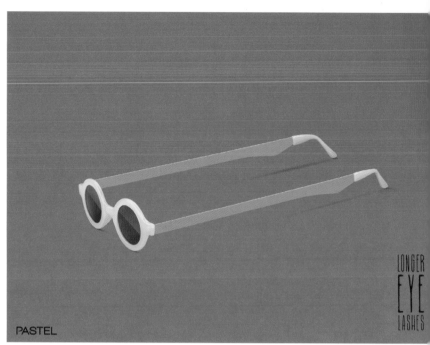

PASTEL

LONGER EYE LASHES

2014

2001
China. By Bates Shanghai *for Estrel Mascara*

2007
Italy. ***Visibly longer lashes*** by JWT Milan *for Coty Italia*

2014
Turkey. ***Longer eye lashes*** by Gode Istanbul *for Pastel Cosmetics*

#fresh-air

Polo. Now with air conditioning as standard.

Das Auto.

2008

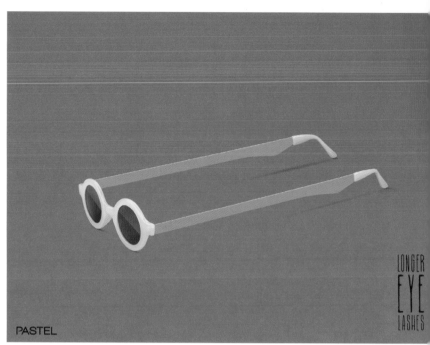

ENJOY FRESHER AIR

2014

2008
Ireland. By Owens DDB *for Volkswagen Polo*

2014
Australia. ***Enjoy fresher air*** by Saatchi & Saatchi Sydney *for Panasonic Automotive Air Conditioning*

YOU LOOK DUMBER WITHOUT GLASSES

+VISION
optical store

2014-A

#selfie-fail

LAFAM OPTICAS

OPHTHALMOLOGY EXAMS 50% OFF

2014-B

drinking-nemo

2002

2004

2005

2013

2015

2002
Mexico. By Ogilvy & Mather
for KFC Big Crunch Inferno

2004
Portugal. By Leo
Burnett Lisbon
for Hot Ketchup Heinz

2005
Singapore. By BBDO
for KFC Hot Devil Drumlets

2013
United States. By Goodby
Silverstein & Partners
San Francisco *for Cheetos
Flamin' Hot Chips*

2015
France. *Oops, that wasn't
the mild chili. Next time
label it* by Rosapark Paris
for Brother

shit-happens

2011

France. *Are you sure your career choice is the best fit?* by Young & Rubicam Paris *for L'étudiant Magazine*

2013

Switzerland. *Solves every washing problem* by Advico Young & Rubicam *for Total Washing Powder*

2008

2008

Shorter commercial breaks

2011

Shorter commercial breaks

2011

2008
Spain.
Downsize your business
by Euro RSCG
for Peugeot Bipper

2011
Chile.
Shorter commercial breaks
by Lowe Porta *for TVN*

2000-A

2000-B

2008

2000-A
Belgium. By GV Company
for *Nivea for Men, Face Care
Clear-Up Strip*

2000-B
Mexico. By Ogilvy & Mather
for *Ponds Clear Pore Strips*

2008
United States. By BBDO
New York *for Venus Razors*

#knocked-out

2006

It's easy to save somebody!

2008

2006
United Kingdom. **Pick up
the phone and stop abuse**
by student work made at
Miami Ad School *for Against
Domestic Violence*

2008
Romania. **Pick up the
phone and save somebody!**
by McCann Erickson *for
Against Domestic Violence*

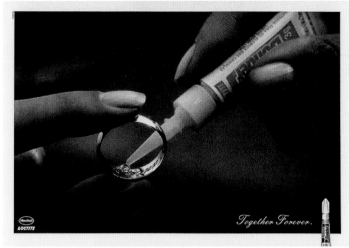

2001

2006

2010

2001
Brazil. *Together forever* by DM9 DDB *for Loctite Glue*

2006
Thailand. By Ogilvy & Mather Bangkok *for Holys Mega Glue Extra Strong*

2010
Portugal. By DDB Lisbon *for Loctite*

1963

just-an-illusion

2000

2010

2013

1963	**2000**	**2010**	**2013**
United States. By DDB *for Volkswagen*	Hungary. By Ogilvy & Mather *for Ford Ka*	Slovenia. By Original *for NLB Bank Car Loans*	Australia. *For Expo, vehicle wraps*

#deep-protest

2008

2001

2001

The Philippines. *Stop overfishing* by BBDO Guerrero Ortega
for WWF Philippines

2008

France. *Stop overfishing* by Ogilvy & Mather Paris
for WWF France

online-news

2009

2007

2007

Saudi Arabia. By Impact BBDO Jeddah
for Saudi Gazette

2009

Poland. By Jasienskistadnicki Warsaw *for Gazeta Wyborcza*

2004

**Anticipate winter.
Volkswagen Winter Check-up.**

2009-A

et si Noël durait toute l'année ?

2009-B

2004
India. By Mudra
Communications
for PARAS DermiCool

2009-A
Italy. By DDB Milan
*for Volkswagen Winter
Check-Up*

2009-B
France. ***What if it was
always christmas?***
by Publicis Conseil
for Orange

#selfie
#fun
#broken

www.yasa.org

8% OF CAR ACCIDENTS HAPPENED WHILE TAKING A SELFIE

yasa Spread the word:
#Last_Driving_selfie

2014

#selfie-and-drive

Don't selfie and drive.

Das Auto.

2015

2014
Saudi Arabia. *Last driving selfie* by Bold Creative Boutique *for YASA*

2015
Mexico. *Don't selfie and drive* by DDB Mexico City *for Volkswagen*

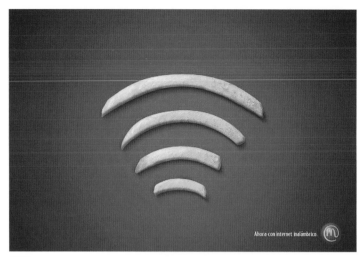

2006

wi-fries

2009

2013

2006
Mexico. *Now with internet*
by RT&A *for McDonald's*

2009
Australia. *Love free wi-fi*
by DDB Sydney
for McDonald's

2013
Spain. *Fries & Wi-Fi*
by TBWA Madrid
for McDonald's

2004

jaws

2007

2004
Germany. *Waterproof*
by Young & Rubicam
for Shark Project

2007
Italy. *Water instinct* by
Young & Rubicam *for Arena*

smile-attack

2007

2011

2007
Germany. *Waterproof*
by Springer & Jacoby Berlin
for Olympus

2011
Austria. *Underwater
camera housings* by Lowe
GGK Vienna *for Hugyfot*

#hang-on

2008

2009

2007

2007
Germany. By TBWA
Düsseldorf *for Gliss Kur
Total Repair Shampoo*

2008
Germany. By Young &
Rubicam Frankfurt *for Activ
Strong Shampoo*

2009
Indonesia. By Fortune *for
Johnny Andrean Shampoo*

#uplifting

2004

2001

2001
France. *With 4 airbags*
by Leo Burnett
for Fiat Punto

2004
United Kingdom. *6 airbags
as standard* by DDB London
for Volkswagen Touran

REALITY SUCKS. utopolis.be

UTOPOLIS
group of cinemas

#ouch

2006

Get movies fast
as never before

Broadband up to 100 Mbit/s

ВОЛЯ
www.volia.com

2012

2006
Belgium. *Reality sucks*
by Duval Guillaume *for*
Utopolis Cinemas

2012
Ukraine. By Scholz & Friends
Kiev *for Volia Broadband*
Internet Provider

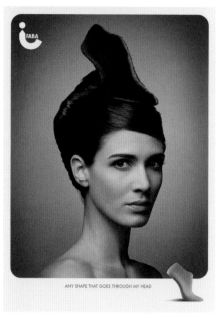

#shoe-obsessed

ANY SHAPE THAT GOES THROUGH MY HEAD

2013

Just what you're looking for.

2008

2008
Argentina. *Just what you're looking for* by Young & Rubicam Buenos Aires *for Alto Palermo Shopping Mall*

2013
Italy. *Any shape that goes through my head* by Mia Comunicazione Milano *for iFaba Shoes*

red-lights-district

2005

Para os fanáticos da cidade.

Novo Tiguan.

2008-A

2008-B

2005
Thailand. *Road is everywhere* by Dentsu Bangkok *for Toyota Hilux*

2008-A
Portugal. By DDB *for Volkswagen Tiguan*

2008-B
Mexico. By BBDO Mexico City *for Jeep*

Stop testing cosmetics on animals   Proefdiervrij

2006

2008

#smells-like-deja-vu

2008

2006
The Netherlands.
***Stop testing cosmetics
on animals*** by Publicis
for *Proefdiervrij*

2008
Germany. By Jung von Matt
Hamburg *for NOAH Against
Animal Testing*

2011

2016

#one-track-mind

2011
UAE. *Censorship tells the wrong story* by Memac Ogilvy Dubai *for Reporters Without Borders*

2016
Costa Rica. *It's not always what it seems* by Grey San Jose *for Hyundai Original Parts*

strong-lookalike

2007

2007
Germany.
Extra strong coffee
by Zebra Werbeagentur
for Rondo Coffee

2008
Germany. *For IO Espresso*

2008

#friendly-sky

2007

2011

2007
Italy. ***Have everyday
a different ceiling***
by Leagas Delaney Milan
for Saab Cabriolet

2011
France. ***Choose your sky***
by Fred & Farid Paris
for Audi A3 Cabriolet

2008

2008

2010

2010

2012

2008
France. By Young & Rubicam
Paris *for Surfrider Calendar*

2010
The Philippines.
By DM9 Jayme Syfu Manila
for Project Runaway

2012
Greece. ***Don't let coastal
pollution become
fashionable*** by Ogilvy &
Mather Athens *for Clean the
Mediterranean*

COPY PASTE **— 183**

food-chain

2010
Santo Domingo. *Trash is the ocean's biggest predator, don't let it destroy our beaches* by Daniel Gonzalez *for Vidazul*

2012
Italy. *Don't compromise the sea and the beach* by Roncaglia & Wijkander Roma *for Marevivo*

2015
Brazil. *We are ocean's biggest predator* by Agência 3 Rio *for Menos Um Lixo*

puzzled

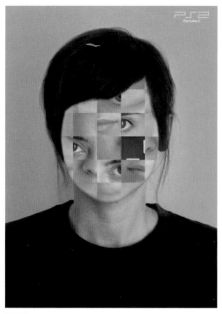

2007

2008

2010

2007
Spain. By TBWA *for Sony Playstation 2*

2008
Sweden. By DDB Stockholm *for McDonald's coffee*

2010
France. *Let's help cancer sufferers rebuild their image* by Leo Burnett Paris *for Mimi Foundation*

2009

2014

look-me-in-the-eyes

2016

2009
United States.
By BBDO Detroit
for Dodge Challenger

2014
United States. *Nice set of double L.E.Ds* by Butler Shine & Stern *for Mini Cooper*

2016
United States. By Widen + Kennedy Portland *for Dodge*

auto-iron

2001

2000

2008

2000
Switzerland. By Studer &
Wohlgemuth *for Swiss Radio*

2001
Denmark. By Saatchi &
Saatchi *for Blockbuster*

2008
India. By Institute of Applied
Art Mumbai *for Easy-On*

#big-splash

The New Volkswagen Touareg.

Accessories shown and features listed may not be part of standard equipment. Images courtesy Photolibrary.

Volkswagen. Das Auto.

2010

2004

2004
France. ***Think big*** by TBWA
Paris *for Nissan Pick-Up*

2010
India. By Mudra DDB *for
Volkswagen Touareg*

manneken-pis

2001

2002

2012

2001

UAE. By Young & Rubicam Dubai *for Ultra Baby Fine Diapers*

2002

Thailand. By BBDO Bangkok *for Drypers Diapers*

2012

Turkey. ***Most absorbent diaper*** by Vietnam agency *for Molfix Diapers*

2003

Long lasting freshness

2006

rearview-check

2008

الآن أريال بعطر الياسمين

2009

2003

The Philippines. By BBDO for Bayer Deodorizer

2006

Egypt. By Saatchi & Saatchi Cairo for Ariel

2008

Austria. By TBWA Vienna for Hansaplast Shoe Freshener

2009

Belgium. *Long lasting freshness* by Saatchi & Saatchi *for Ariel*

2008

2009-A

2009-B

2008
India. **Go wide-angle with Nikon** by JWT *for Cam-Shot*

2009-A
Austria. **Extra wide lens cameras** by Demner, Merlicek & Bergmann *for Leica Shop*

2009-B
India. **Wide angle lenses** by Publicis Gurgaon *for Omax Cameras*

skate-on-board

2005

2007

2014

2005

United States. By Leo
Burnett Chicago *for
McDonald's Tony Hawk's
Tour Sponsorship*

2007

Germany. By Tribal
DDB Hamburg *for Vans
Skateboard Shoes
and Apparel*

2014

Brazil. By Kit Walker
Associates *for X Games*

#fish-breath

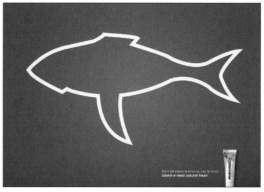

2008

2007

2007

Puerto Rico. By JWT
for Listerine Mouthwash

2008

Austria. **Don't tell everyone
what you had for lunch** by
Saatchi & Saatchi Vienna *for
Blend-a-med*

#fall-season

FAST ACTING PAIN RELIEF

2011

Advil. Faster than pain.

2008

2008

The Netherlands. *Faster than pain* by Publicis for *Advil / Pfizer*

2011

Ukraine. *Fast acting pain relief* by Ogilvy & Mather for *Solpadeine / GlaxoSmithKline*

#torn-apart

2008

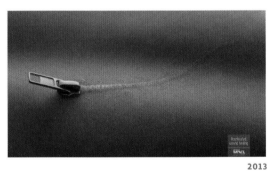

2013

fast-healing

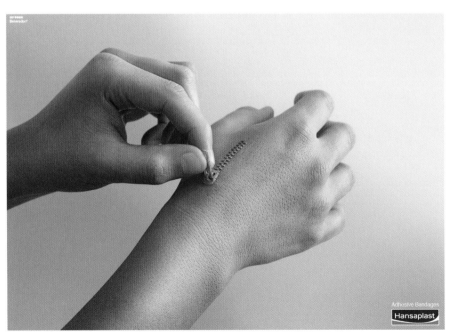

2010

2008
Egypt. **By Strategies Cairo**
for *Suva Accident Prevention*

2014
Ivory Coast. ***Our steel build the cities*** by 6e Sens
for *Sotaci Metallurgy*

2010
Peru. ***Adhesive bandages*** by
TBWA Lima *for Hansaplast*

2013
Singapore. ***Accelerated wound healing*** by McCann
Healthcare *for Impact*

2005

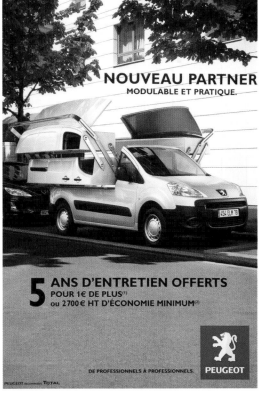

2008

out-of-the-box

2013

2005
Sweden. By Euro RSCG
for *Citroën Utility vehicle*

2008
France. By Euro RSCG BETC
for *Peugeot Partner*

2013
Spain. By Young & Rubicam
Madrid for *Opel Movano*

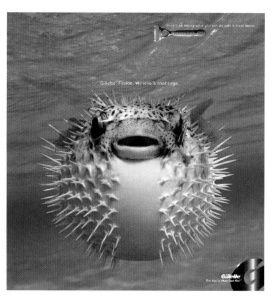

2009

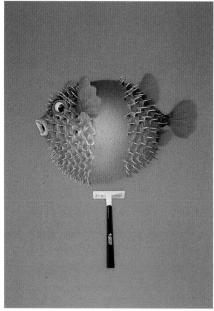

2001

2001

Thailand. By Grey
Worldwide *for Bic Razors*

2009

United States. By BBDO
New York *for Gillette Fusion
Razor (Procter & Gamble)*

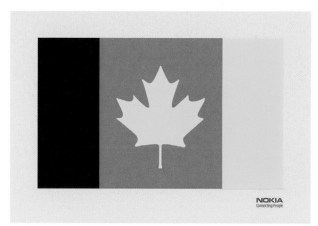

2006

mixed-origins

MÉXICO EN INGLÉS.

harmon hall
the english school

2013

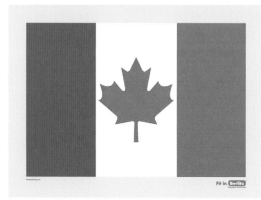

2007

2006

Argentina. By DDB
for Nokia Connecting People

2007

Malaysia. By McCann
Erickson Kuala Lumpur
*for Berlitz Books &
Language School*

2013

Mexico. By Pedro Sugrañes
*for Harmon Hall
English School*

cut-in-two

2001

THE NEW SPEED TRIPLE

TRIUMPH

GO YOUR OWN WAY

2008

2009

2001
Germany. *"Inline-Skates"*
request by Heimat for
Dooyoo Prices Comparator

2008
Germany. By DraftFCB
for *Triumph*

2009
Belgium. By Duval Guillaume
Antwerp for *Lazer Bicycle
Helmets*

2007-B

#break-the-glass

2007-A

2007-A
New Zealand. By Clemenger
BBDO *for ALAC (Alcohol
Advisory Council) helpsite
hadenough.org.nz*

2007-B
The Netherlands. By Roorda
for Alcohol Info Helpline

modern-father

2002

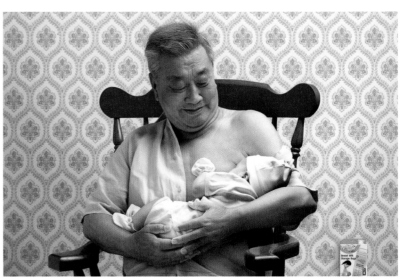

2012

2002
France. **Women are only
interested in their car** by
Bates *for Seat Arosa*

2012
Thailand. By Mohallem
Artplan *for Nanny Breast
Milk Storage Bag*

2013

#final-countdown

2015

2013

Canada. ***Days until it's back*** by Leo Burnett Toronto *for "The Walking Dead"*

2015

Denmark. ***Days left*** by Seligemig Copenhagen *for HBO Nordic, "Game Of Thrones"*

2006

2006

For your stylish hair

2014

#hair-dress-her

2014

2006
Germany.
The haircare collection
by Grey Düsseldorf
for Pantene Pro-V Haircare

2014
Indonesia.
For your stilish hair
by Matari Jakarta
for Lucido-L Haircare

#never-sleep

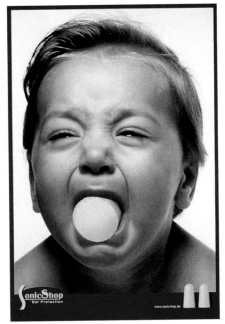

2001

2001
Germany. By Scholz &
Friends Berlin *for Sonic Shop
Ear Protections*

2008
Thailand. By Monday
Bangkok *for A-Tap Earplugs*

2008

2009

bedside-lamp

2008
Germany. By KNSK
for Evonik Chemicals

2009
Morocco. *Long lasting
whiteness* by JWT
for Trident

20th January 1999. First Hebrew Cinema Film Festival. ✡

1999

7ᵗʰ JEWISH FILM FESTIVAL

2003

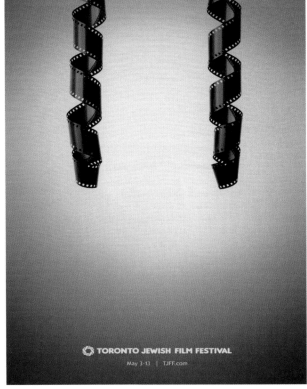

TORONTO JEWISH FILM FESTIVAL
May 3-13 | TJFF.com

2012

#jewish-film

1999
Italy. By This is a thing
for *Hebrew Film Festival*

2003
Brazil. By DDB São Paulo
for the *7ᵗʰ Jewish
Film Festival*

2012
Canada. By BBDO
for the *Jewish Film Festival*

not-so-fresh

2005

2005
United States. By Saatchi &
Saatchi New York *for Tide*

2008

2008
Singapore. By Leo Burnett
for Fab Perfect

#made-in-china

2005

2006

2013

2005
Austria. By BBDO Vienna
for Suzi Wan Hot Sauce

2006
United States. By DDB
Dallas *for Tabasco
Hot Sauce*

2013
Turkey. ***Extra hot shrimps***
by BigBang Istanbul
for Jong Hwa Restaurant

Easily removes the most difficult stains.

2008-A

removal

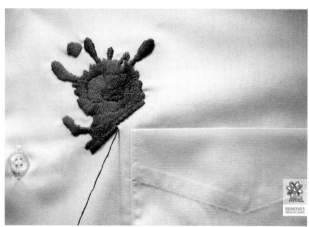

2008-B

2008-A

Brazil. *Easily removes the most difficult stains* by Euro RSCG São Paulo *for Vanish*

2008-B

Romania. *Removes dried-in stains* by Saatchi & Saatchi Bucharest *for Ariel*

2006

#old-fart

2009

2011

2006

The Netherlands. By FHV
BBDO for *Strip Dagen
Cartoons Exhibition*

2009

China. By DDB *for TianTian
Air Freshener*

2011

Thailand. By TBWA Bangkok
for *3M Air Purifier*

poop

2002

2005

2002
Belgium. By McCann Erickson *for Reckitt Benckiser Scholl Shoe Refreshener*

2005
The Philippines. ***No more smelly clothes*** by Ace Saatchi & Saatchi *for Ariel (Procter & Gamble)*

#eyes-opener

2011

2014

2011
Ukraine. By BBDO Kiev *for Pepsi Max with Ginseng*

2014
Peru. By Circus Grey Lima *for Volt Energy Drink*

1997

#alien-propaganda

2007

2008

1997
France. *Famous brands at unbelievable prices* by Euro RSCG BETC *for Galeries Lafayette Department Store*

2007
Spain. *Nobody will believe you've seen a price like it* by Contrapunto Madrid *for Smart*

2008
Sweden. By Åkestam Holst *for Magic Sunday Advertising Package*

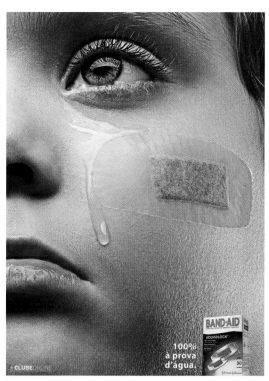

2008

2009

#waterproof

2008
Brazil. *Waterproof*
by JWT *for Band-Aid*

2009
Thailand. *Waterproof
plasters* by McCann
Erickson Bangkok *for Boots*

wiper-concerto

2008

2011

2008
Tunisia. By Memac Ogilvy
Label Tunis *for CMIJ Violin
Lessons Flyer*

2011
Sweden. *Windscreen wiper
violin* by Frank & Earnest *for
Yamaha Violins Flyer*

2013

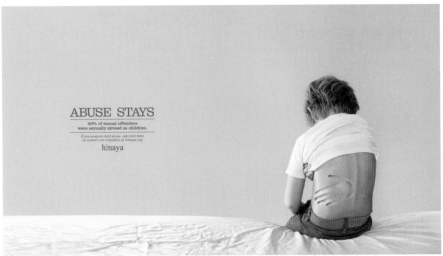

2013

#touching

2015

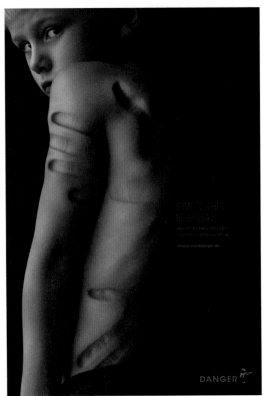

2015

2013
UAE / Lebanon. ***Abuse stays***
by Leo Burnett *for Himaya
Against Child Abuse*

2015
Germany. ***Some touches
never leave*** by Publicis
Hamburg *for Innocence
in Danger*

2006

2009

2014

2006

China. ***Not only a tree is cut down*** by Saatchi & Saatchi Guangzhou *for Greenpeace*

2009

Germany. By BBDO *for Rettet Den Regenwald*

2014

India. ***When the wood go, wildlife goes*** by Ganesh Prasad Acharya (freelance work) *for Sanctuary*

not-new

SUDDENLY, EVERYTHING ELSE SEEMS OLD. MINI

2014

NEW MÉGANE COUPÉ. EVERYTHING ELSE SEEMS OLDER.

2008

2008

France. *Everything else seems older* by Publicis Conseil *for Renault Megane*

2014

Canada. *Suddenly, everything else seems old* by Anomaly Toronto *for Mini*

FUJIFILM

2006

FINEPIX

FUJIFILM

2006

#anti-shake

Enjoy the anti-shake mode.

SAMSUNG

SAMSUNG L100

2008

2006

Brazil. *With anti-shake system* by DPZ Propaganda *for Fujifilm Finepix*

2008

India. *Enjoy the anti-shake mode* by Cheil Worldwide New Delhi *for Samsung L730*

2008

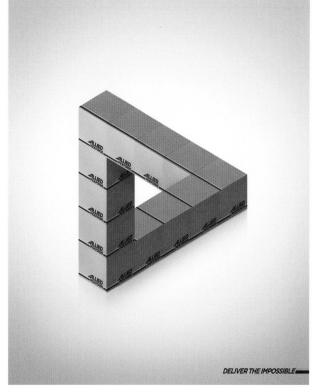

penrose-triangle

DELIVER THE IMPOSSIBLE

2011

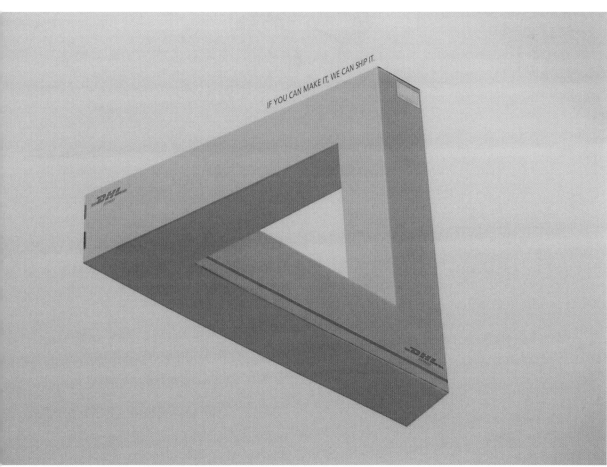

IF YOU CAN MAKE IT, WE CAN SHIP IT.

2013

2005

2005

2005

remixed

2007

www.vinylexchange.co.uk
0161 228 1122

music lives vinyl exchange

2012

2007

2005
Argentina. By Kepel & Mata
for Musimundo Music Stores

2007
France. **Make your mix**
by Agence V
for Neuf Music

2012
United Kingdom.
By Propaganda Leeds
for Vinyl Exchange

COPY PASTE — **213**

ADVERTISING & COPYCATS

WHAT DOES THE LAW SAY?

JOE TALKS TO ÉLISABETH MARRACHE, LAWYER

En

Is there any specific law applicable to advertising creations?

"No, there is no specific law as such. However, such creations are protected in many countries by copyright law, trademark law, industrial design rights and unfair competition legislation. There are also a number of specific regulations applicable to certain types of advertising campaigns (adverts targeting young people, promotional campaigns sale of certain products regulated by law [i.e. alcool, medicinal products...] etc.).

Which creations are liable to protection?

"All advertising creations are eligible for copyright protection provided that the creations are original and materialised on a certain medium. The concept of originality is, however, difficult to appreciate, as it means that the creation reflects its author's personality. For example, an advert showing 'before/after' photos of women to advertise slimming products cannot be considered original. From a practical point of view, the author must have shown a certain creativity, for instance via a certain setting or a different slogan.

There is also the possibility of protecting a logo or slogan through trademark law or industrial design rights when a graphic creation is involved. In this case, the agency must ensure that its slogan is not misleading with regard to the quality, origin or nature of the product concerned and that it is not a description of the promoted product. For example, it would be impossible to register the slogan 'Using our washing powder, stains disappear', but 'Rowenta your life' or 'Just do it' can be protected.

Is it possible to protect my idea to ensure that it is not used by a competitor?

"Advertising ideas and topics cannot be appropriated by a single person. For instance, whiteness is a topic that cannot be claimed by a sole producer, as it would give him a competitive advantage over the rest of the market, as seen in the famous Procter&Gamble case and confirmed several times by courts. In reality, to be able to claim protection, the creation has to be 'materialised' in a developed form, though not finalised, i.e. the blueprints or just the project presentation documents suffice to benefit from protection.

How can I protect myself, making sure that what I have created is not just a reproduction of another agency's work?

"In France, with the exception of actually registering a slogan or a logo as a trademark, advertising creations are not listed in an official register. But there are three things I recommend in order to avoid being surprised:
→ check the adverts database to make sure that what you have created does not reproduce the work of another agency;
→ inform the client that the content of the media presented is protected by copyright;
→ have the client sign a non-disclosure agreement before disclosing any documentation, with a promise that it will not be used in the case the agency is not selected. This recommendation is, however, difficult to put into practice as the negotiating margin is often limited at this moment of the pitch process.

Who actually owns advertising creations?

"In most cases, advertising creations belong to communications agencies who then contractually assign their copyrights to the client. In common law countries, the work done by agency employees automatically belongs to the agency. This is less simple in France, where there is a tendency to protect employees and freelance authors. In practice, there are two situations: first, where it is not possible to identify the personal contributions of each of the authors involved in an advertising campaign (e.g. the photographer, the graphic designer, marketing team) the creation will be considered as a "collective work" and copyrights will be ab initio vested with the agency. In the opposite case, the agency must ensure that it has obtained the intellectual property rights from its employees and service providers via a written intellectual property assignment clause.

What are the risks for copycats?

"Any use of a protected work requires the authorisation of the copyright holder. An advertising author reproducing a large amount of an already existing creation risks being sued on civil and criminal grounds. Said author is likely to pay damages for unfair competition and commercial free-riding. The fact that the plagiarist has done so in good faith, unintentionally imitating something or unfairly competing doesn't really count. All that matters is that he has broken the law.

Of course, the purpose of copyright law is not to censor advertising campaigns that look alike, as certain formulas are necessary for describing a product and a client cannot appropriate them. Courts rule on a case-by-case basis, examining the work done by the author, looking at its originality, the differences and the risk of the public being confused.

Who is liable?

"Liability is primarily held by the client under whose name the advertising campaign is disclosed. However, in the case of a legal dispute, the client may call the agency as a guarantor, as it was responsible for designing an ad not infringing third parties' rights." ∎

PUBLICITÉ & PLAGIAT

QUE DIT LA LOI?

JOE PARLE À ÉLISABETH MARRACHE, AVOCATE

Fr

Existe-t-il un droit spécifique applicable aux créations publicitaires?

«Non, il n'existe pas de droit propre aux créations publicitaires en tant que tel. Toutefois, ces créations sont protégées dans de nombreux pays par le droit de la propriété littéraire et artistique, le droit des marques, des dessins et modèles et l'action en concurrence déloyale.

Il existe également des réglementations spécifiques applicables à certains types de campagnes publicitaires (messages destinés à la jeunesse, opérations promotionnelles, vente de produits réglementés [p. ex. alcools, médicaments…] etc.).

Quelles sont les créations protégeables?

«Toutes les créations publicitaires sont protégées à partir du moment où elles sont originales et qu'elles ont été matérialisées sur un support.

La notion d'originalité est difficile à apprécier, car elle signifie que la création revêt l'empreinte de la personnalité de l'auteur. Par exemple, une publicité représentant deux photographies de femmes avec la mention 'avant/après' pour commercialiser des produits amincissants ne peut être considérée comme originale. D'un point de vue pratique, le publicitaire doit faire preuve d'une certaine créativité, prévoir une mise en scène ou une accroche différente.

Il est également possible de protéger un logo ou un slogan par le droit des marques ou par le droit des dessins et modèles lorsqu'il s'agit d'une création graphique. Dans ce cas, l'agence devra veiller à ce que sa marque n'induise pas le public en erreur sur la qualité, l'origine ou la nature du produit et qu'elle ne soit pas descriptive du produit promu. Par exemple, il n'est pas possible de déposer 'Avec notre lessive, les taches disparaissent', mais une marque comme 'Rowentez-vous la vie' ou 'Just do it' est protégeable.

Est-il possible de protéger mon idée pour m'assurer qu'elle ne sera pas reprise par un concurrent?

«Les idées et les thèmes publicitaires ne peuvent pas faire l'objet d'une appropriation par une seule personne. Par exemple, le thème de la blancheur ne peut être l'apanage d'un seul fabricant, car cela reviendrait à lui conférer un avantage anticoncurrentiel sur le marché. Cette solution a été retenue dans un célèbre arrêt Procter&Gamble et réaffirmée à plusieurs reprises.

En réalité, pour pouvoir prétendre à une protection, il est nécessaire que la création ait été 'matérialisée', peu importe qu'elle soit finalisée. Ainsi, les rushes, les roughs ou les simples documents de présentation de projet permettent de bénéficier d'une protection.

Comment se protéger et s'assurer que sa création ne reproduit pas le travail d'une autre agence?

«En France, sauf en cas de dépôt du slogan ou du logo à titre de marque, les créations publicitaires ne sont pas répertoriées dans un registre officiel. Trois mesures sont toutefois préconisées pour s'éviter de mauvaises surprises:
→ consulter les bases de données publicitaires afin de s'assurer que sa création ne reproduit pas le travail d'une autre agence;
→ informer l'annonceur que le contenu des supports remis lors de la présentation est protégé par le droit d'auteur;
→ faire signer aux annonceurs un engagement de confidentialité sur le projet présenté avec promesse de ne pas utiliser le projet si l'agence n'est pas sélectionnée. Cette recommandation est toutefois difficile à mettre en pratique, car la marge de négociation est souvent limitée à cette étape du processus de sélection d'une agence.

À qui appartiennent les créations publicitaires?

«Les créations publicitaires appartiennent le plus souvent aux agences de communication qui cèdent ensuite leurs droits par contrat à l'annonceur. Dans les pays de common law, le travail réalisé par les salariés des agences appartient automatiquement aux agences. La solution n'est pas aussi évidente en France, qui a tendance à être assez favorable aux salariés et auteurs free-lances. En pratique, deux situations sont possibles: la première, où il n'est pas possible d'identifier la part de travail de chaque intervenant dans le processus créatif (photographe, graphiste, commerciaux…), la création sera qualifiée d'œuvre collective et l'agence sera alors investie des droits dès leur origine. Dans le cas contraire, l'agence devra s'assurer avoir obtenu les droits de ses salariés et prestataires par le biais d'une clause de cession de droits.

Quels sont les risques du plagiat?

«Toute utilisation d'une œuvre protégée requiert l'autorisation du titulaire des droits et l'auteur d'une publicité reproduisant en grande partie une création précédente s'expose à des poursuites civiles et pénales pour contrefaçon et à une action en responsabilité pour concurrence déloyale et parasitisme.

Il importe peu que le plagiaire soit de bonne foi, celle-ci étant inopérante en matière de contrefaçon et de concurrence déloyale où seule la faute compte (même si elle s'avère non intentionnelle).

Bien entendu, il n'est pas question de condamner toute ressemblance entre deux campagnes publicitaires, car certaines formules sont nécessaires à la description d'un produit et un annonceur ne saurait se les approprier. Les tribunaux apprécient au cas par cas en analysant le travail effectué par le créatif, l'originalité, les différences et le risque de confusion auprès du public.

Qui sera responsable?

«Le premier responsable est l'annonceur sous le nom duquel est diffusée la campagne publicitaire. Toutefois, en cas de litige, l'annonceur pourra appeler en garantie l'agence de publicité chargée de concevoir la campagne publicitaire qui aurait dû concevoir une campagne à l'abri de tout risque.» ∎

GLOSSARY

Coincidence

The act of coinciding, taking place at the same time or being identical in terms of time and duration. Fortuitous simultaneity.

Counterfeit

Forgery, copy. Fraudulent reproduction of a work. Caricatured imitation. Illegal imitation or reproduction of a work by a third party.

Copy

Faithful reproduction or imitation of an original document or work.

Creation

Act consisting of producing or forming a being or thing which did not previously exist.

Cryptomnesia

From the Greek *kruptos* meaning "hidden" or "secret" and *mnémè* meaning "memory" or "recollection", literally "hidden recollection", is a memory mechanism whereby a person has the false recollection of having produced a thought (idea, advertising creation), when this thought was actually produced by another person. Cryptomnesia can lead to involuntary plagiarism experienced in the author's memory which the latter cannot distinguish from a new inspiration.

Imitation

Act of using something as a model. Parody extending as far as caricature. Work inspired by another work. Work without originality. Reproduction of something with the aim of its being accepted as the original.

Twin

Identical items which have been or appear to have been made to go together (either positioned symmetrically or in parallel or forming part of the same element). Duplicate. An item which is a physical or moral replica (with varying degrees of precision) of another.

Parody

Work with a satirical or comic purpose which imitates a known work in part or in its entirety by making it appear ridiculous. Vulgar imitation which only replicates certain elements.

Parasitism

Term used in competition law to refer to the attitude of a firm which, even though it is involved in a different field of business, usurps the notoriety or techniques used by a renowned firm.

Pastiche

Literary or artistic work in which the style or manner of a writer or artist is imitated either with the intention of deceiving or for a satirical purpose.

Plagiarism

Work consisting of borrowed elements; reproduction of an original work or part thereof without admission. A plagiarist wrongly claims authorship of a work by reproducing it, with varying degrees of precision, and presenting it as his personal creation.

Presumption of innocence

Attitude to be adopted initially when facing an obvious offence with regard to a similarity between different adverts. *"Everyone is presumed innocent until they have been found guilty."* This means that everyone is to be considered not guilty unless evidence of their guilt is found.

Recycling

Transformation or refining of an object or work so that it can be reused. Complete alteration of something.

Reminiscence

This is the most dangerous form of borrowing as it appears to be produced subconsciously. Spontaneous act whereby the author subconsciously imitates the work of another person to which he has been exposed at some point in the past and of which his memory has retained a trace without his being able to recognise the source. A convenient excuse for plagiarism.

LEXIQUE

Coïncidence

Fait de coïncider, d'avoir lieu en même temps, d'être identique en date ou en durée. Simultanéité fortuite.

Contrefaçon

Faux, copie. Reproduction frauduleuse d'une œuvre. Imitation caricaturale. Imitation ou reproduction illicite de l'œuvre d'autrui.

Copie

Reproduction ou imitation fidèle d'un document ou d'une œuvre originale.

Création

Acte consistant à produire ou à former un être ou une chose qui n'existait pas auparavant.

Cryptomnésie

Du grec *kruptos* «caché», «secret» et *mnémè* «mémoire», «souvenir», littéralement «souvenir caché», est un biais mémoriel par lequel une personne a le souvenir erroné d'avoir produit une pensée (une idée, une création publicitaire), alors que cette pensée a été en réalité produite par quelqu'un d'autre. La cryptomnésie peut conduire au plagiat involontaire dont l'auteur fait une expérience mnésique qu'il ne peut distinguer d'une inspiration nouvelle.

Imitation

Action de prendre pour modèle. Parodie qui va jusqu'à la caricature. Œuvre inspirée d'une autre œuvre. Œuvre sans originalité. Reproduction de quelque chose dont on veut faire passer la copie pour vraie.

Jumeau

Qui sont identiques et sont ou semblent faits pour aller de pair (soit placés symétriquement ou parallèlement, soit faisant partie constitutive d'un même ensemble). Double. Qui est la réplique physique ou morale (plus ou moins fidèle) d'un autre.

Parodie

Œuvre qui, à des fins satiriques ou comiques, imite en la tournant en ridicule une partie ou la totalité d'une œuvre connue. Imitation grossière qui ne restitue que certaines apparences.

Parasitisme

Employé dans le droit de la concurrence pour désigner l'attitude d'une entreprise qui, bien qu'elle exerce une activité dans un domaine différent, usurpe la notoriété ou les techniques qu'emploie une entreprise de renom.

Pastiche

Œuvre littéraire ou artistique dans laquelle on imite le style, la manière d'un écrivain, d'un artiste, soit dans l'intention de tromper, soit dans une intention satirique.

Plagiat

Œuvre faite d'emprunts; reproduction non avouée d'une œuvre originale ou d'une partie de cette dernière. Un plagiaire s'attribue abusivement la paternité en reproduisant, avec plus ou moins de fidélité, une œuvre que l'on présente comme personnelle.

Présomption d'innocence

Attitude à adopter de prime abord face à un flagrant délit de ressemblance entre deux pubs. «*Tout homme est présumé innocent jusqu'à ce qu'il ait été reconnu coupable.*» Ce qui signifie que toute personne est considérée comme non coupable tant qu'une preuve de sa culpabilité n'a pas été retenue.

Recyclage

Transformation, épuration d'un objet ou d'une œuvre en vue de permettre sa réutilisation. Modification complète de quelque chose.

Réminiscence

Le type d'emprunt le plus dangereux, car censé être produit par l'inconscient. Acte irréfléchi par lequel l'auteur imite inconsciemment l'œuvre d'un autre dont il a eu connaissance à une époque plus ou moins reculée, et dont sa mémoire a gardé le souvenir sans qu'il puisse cependant en reconnaître la source. Excuse commode pour un plagiat.

INDEX